# THE CONCRETE CEILING

By Margaret Marshall-Bucklew

HIS Publishing Group is a division of Human Improvement Specialists, llc. For information, visit www.hispubg.com or contact the publisher at info@hispubg.com

ISBN: 979-8-218-94811-5 *paperback*

*The author and publisher specifically disclaim all responsibility for any liability, loss or risk, personal or otherwise, that is incurred as a consequence, directly or indirectly, of the use and application of any of the contents of this book. Some names and identifying details have been changed to protect the privacy of individuals.*

Division of Human Improvement Specialists, llc.
www.hispubg.com | *info@hispubg.com*

# CONTENTS

# INTRODUCTION

This book is based on the true story of a woman who never gave up. It tells of the long journey she took from prejudice. Barbara Walters could be in the same category because she was the first woman news commentator. Sexual harassment was commonplace. Women were hostages to their mundane jobs and lifestyles. Most were secretaries and married at a young age. This book covers the challenges that women faced at the end of the 20th century. It's also a joyful reminder that persistence, respect, and hard work can give you advancement and credibility. There are many stories of females climbing to the top. It's hard to imagine a world where women are respected for their abilities, hard work, and educational backgrounds. May we continue to evolve and accept each other for our abilities, not by gender but by merit.

# CHAPTER 1

## DALLAS AND THE MAGIC BEANS

Be present, not perfect.

"Marty," called Ruth Bledsoe, Marty's mother, "You have a pleasant!"

From an early age, Marty called presents, "pleasants."

She ran to the metal screen door as it slammed to see what had come in the mail. Her namesake, Aunt Marty Brew, always showered her with gifts on her birthday, for special achievements, and on Hanukkah. But on her sweet 16th, Aunt Marty gifted her shares of Standard Oil of New Jersey. What a pleasant!

She did not yet understand the concept of dividends, so her older brother, Vic, explained them to her. Marty was in awe of what they represented. She thought it was a great idea to get checks every three months, regardless of what the certificates meant. She thought, "Maybe someday I will be a stockbroker and understand all about them."

After graduating from Poplar Bluff High School in a small rural farming community in Southeast Missouri, Aunt Marty gave her a silver tea service. Thinking it was a random gift with no potential for revenue, Marty packed it up and stored it in the closet. Cash was king, and the dividends had hit the spot. She was hooked. Vic was right.

Aunt Marty suggested the stock dividends be used to help her through college. However, the dividends were not spent on books or tuition. Marty was a clotheshorse and decided to build her wardrobe instead. Her best friend from high school, Shauna Jones, was always happy to wear anything from her wardrobe, even though Shauna was a foot shorter. Trading clothes was a way of life for everyone because it helped diversify their looks and fit their budgets.

Stoddard, her second bestie, however, was far too tall and lanky to join in the clothes-sharing. Her arms were quite a bit longer, and her legs were like two columns that you would see at the Parthenon.

The seed of the world of stocks had been firmly planted in Marty. Dividends were like magic beans. Marty was now a shareholder, and the more she learned, the more she wanted to be involved in the lucrative world of stocks.

On January 1, 1973, Exxon was formed, replacing Standard Oil of New Jersey and increasing its share count. Marty now felt like an oil baroness and tried to buy only Exxon gas from then on. She owned a piece of it, so why not support the company? Her dad always said, "Invest in things you use." Wise old bird that he was.

Her dad, Louis Bledsoe, was a closed book. The Sam Walton of Poplar Bluff, Missouri, where Marty grew up. He didn't want anyone to know about his daughters' windfall. He didn't even consult with Marty about the shares. He felt that discussing money was taboo in the Bledsoe household. It was beneath them. Instead, her new certificates arrived in the mail without fanfare, and she was unaware of what happened to the shares or where they were kept. Louis kept everything in a safety deposit box at the bank. No telling how much he had hidden away.

They received more shares after Exxon split. Again, her dad said nothing. There was no explanation, so Marty assumed she had been awarded more shares by osmosis. However, the stage was now set for the ever-so-curious girl. She thought it was thrilling how stocks and dividends provided freedom, and she loved it. Her dream career was to be a wildly successful stockbroker with a diamond-encrusted watch or a genuine Rolex. One day, when she owned her own mansion, money would be talked about A LOT!

## DALLAS HERE WE COME

After graduating from college at Southeast Missouri State University in Cape Girardeau, Missouri, Marty and her bestie, Stoddard, were so ready to leave their small town. They both had attended college, home of the not-fighting Indians. Tuition was cheap, and they earned a degree. That's all that mattered to Marty, for she wanted to be a professional and wear a business suit and a white, starched blouse, just like a man.

The two vowed to move to Dallas and wanted to be right in the heart of its singles scene, near Greenville Avenue and Meadow Road. Everything of interest to them would be close, and that meant not having to venture out onto the intimidating Central Expressway, I-75, or Central, as everyone called it. Being from a small town in Missouri, Marty had little to no experience navigating the giant highways. Dallas was too alluring not to move there, though. The men, the jobs, and the clothes. Who could resist?

Stoddard, a tall, slim, naturally curly-haired blonde who went by her last name, was Marty's best friend. Her first name was Cathy, with a C. She was a tall, strong, big-boned girl of German descent. Marty was careful not to describe her that way because Stoddard took the term "big boned" as a complete and utter insult. She saw herself only as a tall girl, which she was, except that it had its disadvantages when it came to finding respect from her many suitors.

Marty and Stoddard met one snowy night in Cape Girardeau, and they immediately felt sisterhood. Neither girl had visions of weddings, children, or baggage. Hell no. It was time to fly, and fly for peanuts they did, which was a slogan for the Dallas-based Southwest Airlines at the time.

They booked flights to Dallas from St. Louis and secured a crash pad with Marty's older brother, Stan Bledsoe, who lived in Plano, Texas, just north of Dallas. The crash pad was the perfect scene for two party girls. The place was free and all they could afford on this trip.

Louis and Ruth Bledsoe were on the trip, too, looking for a suitable place for Marty. Little did they know apartment finders were a joke and a rip-off, but Marty zeroed right in on the sexy single part of town. No one in Dallas, except Marty's big brother Stan, seemed to be married. She figured if she zoomed in on the

Greenville Avenue area, which was just far enough away from the SMU college crowd, she could land in Mecca, and she did.

Apartments were grouped by demographic eligibility, so Marty and Stoddard circled in on lower Greenville Avenue at Meadow Road. It was known to be affordable for singles, and the men were everywhere. Plus, Northpark Mall was only one exit away on I-75, a perfect combination of men and shopping.

The apartment they planned to live in was just off the Interstate that split Dallas in half, running north and south, so they wouldn't have to venture much farther than where they were living. Coming from small Missouri towns, the girls were intimidated by the traffic. With NorthPark Mall being so close, all their needs were met…bars, men, and shopping. Did they need anything else?

Marty called her boss in Missouri and told him she was moving to Dallas. Frank Mayberry graciously responded, "I tell you what, if you return and work through the summer, I will give you a thumbs up for unemployment." The next day, the two of them boarded a plane and flew back to Missouri.

## MISSOURI - UNFINISHED BUSINESS

Many nights in Cape Girardeau, they drank, partied, and danced until the Mule Lip Saloon closed. Then, they ventured across the river, where the bars, specifically the Purple Crackle, would greet them with another full four hours of possibilities. Cocaine was everywhere, so it wasn't hard to keep up with the crowd.

They both smoked pot every day. It was common practice to be stoned. Missouri had an abundant supply of weed due to the many accomplished growers. The dark, rich soil and frequent rainstorms made the land perfect for strains of marijuana that could make you high as a kite. Add that to a beer bust in the woods somewhere, and you have the combination for the perfect party.

Another bar they frequented closer to campus was The Endzone. This establishment was their go-to for happy hour because beer was $ 0.25 a glass. Rarely did either girl pay for their drinks, but it helped to know that if they did have to pay, it was affordable.

One particular visit stood out in Marty's mind. Stoddard admitted she had slept with Leven Roth, Marty's current conquest. A bathroom shout-out sent both girls packing to their respective corners, but tempers smoothed over with the promise of a " hands off" policy. Once either girl had started seeing someone, the other girl could not sleep with them. The girl code was established and abided by, so the girls continued their merrymaking.

Marty's part-time job was at The General Store, owned by Frank Mayberry. Frank was famous for being a wild man who would try anything to make a buck. His sister store, The Fox Hole, adjoined his other store and carried used army goods. The General Store, however, was a head shop. Its name was a perfect camouflage for what was sold there.

Marty was quite popular with the druggies because of her job at The General Store. Her parents had no idea what kind of store it was. Her license plate was I-BONG, which she told her parents, stood for "I Will Better Our National Government."

It worked, and they never knew the truth about the license plate. If they had known, they would have disowned her, good Jews that they were.

Marty could supply rolling papers and coke spoons or grinders for the hard-to-chop cocaine. Glass mirrors for spreading the coke were always a handy tool to disperse the white powder. Once, Stoddard and Marty went to a party where there was a line of coke crafted into a spiral that looked like it was from outer space. Someone had Quaaludes, the giant pills that made you feel like melting goo, but the coke medicated that effect. The party lasted all night and into the next day, but the crash was hard.

One night, Stoddard and Marty waltzed into the Mule Lip Saloon, halter tops, and hip huggers on, and decided to have a "who could drink more tequila shots" challenge. Stoddard won, but she did her famous blackout routine when they arrived at their shared rental just off campus. She passed out right as they were entering the front door and slowly drifted backwards until she fell flat on her back.

Stoddard could cook all day, party all night until she puked, and then party some more. When she threw up, she was so ladylike that it sounded as if she was saying, "I'm calling Roy." Marty grabbed her by the feet and dragged her into the house, left her in the front room, then ran to the bathroom so she, too, could call "Roy."

Roy became their secret code word when they got sick. The next day, both girls felt like dog doodoo, so they had Bloody Marys to recover, and by noon, they were off to Pink Rocks to enjoy the river, sun, and more partying.

## THAT WAS IT FOR MISSOURI

Marty had done exactly as Frank asked, honoring her commitment over the summer. But now was the time for her to make a gracious exit from Missouri. She was looking forward to all the opportunities Dallas offered, not to mention the abundance of eligible rich men.

She was ready to move to the big city, so she loaded up her Cutlass from top to bottom. She had two cats, Ruffy and Tuffy, and they had never been in a car, so it was hard to tell how they would do. She brought along their litter box just to be safe.

When she arrived to pick up Stoddard, she had everything packed and ready to go. The two of them finally hit the road heading for Dallas, and the summer of 1979 was just a blur in the rear-view mirror.

It wasn't long after they arrived in Dallas that Marty secured a job as an assistant manager at The Tannery West, a high-end leather specialty store, hoping to move into management. It was in North Park Mall, so the commute was easy. She worked hard to become the big boss because the store's merchandise attracted a very exclusive clientele. A pair of black leather pants sold for $200, and Marty immediately put them on layaway using her employee discount.

The band Hall & Oates showed up one evening looking for leather jackets. Marty was so excited she could hardly remember her sales tactics. The hell with selling, rock 'n' roll had arrived at her doorstep.

Within six months, Marty was promoted to manager and had several ideas to boost sales, including hosting impromptu fashion shows at the elite private nightclub, Elan. Her models would be her employees. Stoddard had secured a cocktail waitress position at Elan and thus opened the door to the swanky nightclub for her bestie to show off The Tannery West's goods.

People who frequented Elan were the who's who in Dallas: the Dallas Cowboys players Hollywood Henderson and TooTall Jones, the cast of the popular Friday night sequel Dallas, and local elites like Ross Perot and family. The club was arranged with nooks and crannies for private socializing, backgammon, and snorting lines of coke. Everyone was indulging and drugs were everywhere. Quaaludes and weed were the come-down drugs and were plentiful. Marty and Stoddard couldn't resist the offers for drugs and fell headlong into partying.

Marty learned through trial and error that men could fake being rich. Many of these pseudo-rich types belonged to and frequented the private clubs like the Playboy Club and Elan.

However, they wore fake Rolexes and had plenty of cocaine to lure their female prey. The girls were on to them and knew who the real players were.

One day, Stan called Marty and asked if she and Stoddard would like to come over after work, stay the night, and spend the next day with the kids. Marty thought it was a great idea. Stan had two young kids, Hillary and Jon, whom she adored.

That night, Stoddard waited on the owner of all the local Denny's restaurants. He went by JoJo, but he didn't look like a JoJo, because he was a very large, round, and short man. His sidekick or bodyguard, who was a sight for sore eyes, requested that Stoddard give them free tequila shots all night in exchange for bumps. Bumps were one hit of cocaine (coke).

JoJo asked Stoddard if she could come over to his house after her shift, and he offered to take her in his limo. Stoddard told Marty, and a plan was hatched. Neither girl had ridden in a limo before, so they climbed in and opened every drawer and canister inside the car. There was champagne and real flutes, so they poured two glasses and clinked them. Then they motioned to the driver, and off they went to JoJo's house.

Upon arrival, Jojo was in his robe and doling out party favors; lines of coke and lots of weed. Marty rolled joints, her special talent, having previously managed a head shop in Missouri. That was her first real job.

Then, the enemy showed up: other girls. The balance was upset with the presence of two other girls, and Marty and Stoddard wondered why they had been invited. Little did they know or suspect that JoJo was planning threesomes for him and his bodyguard. Nor did they know what crack was.

Crack cocaine was smoked, and neither girl ever turned down something free for the first time, except heroin. That decision was a big mistake, or their saving grace. Marty was so stoned she couldn't take any more hits and requested the driver take her home. She gave him Stan's address. Stoddard stayed behind with Rocco, the bodyguard, and the girls after Marty had left.

The next day, Marty's toddler nephew, John, yelled, "Mom, Dad, Aunt Marty's friend is getting out of a big black car, and she's not wearing her shoes."

Stoddard was fully dressed, carrying her heels, and looking like she'd been up all night. In fact, both girls had been up all night. The effect of the crack had been way too much. They both vowed never to do crack again. They had smoked some marijuana in hopes it might mitigate the impact, but to no avail. Only time would ease the effects. Marty experienced a crash the next day, which was the worst. Marty wished she'd been able to throw up to get rid of the feeling but hadn't been able to call "Roy."

Stoddard's entrance had gone over like a turd in a punch bowl, and Stan told Marty that Stoddard had to go. Stoddard called Rocco, and the limo reappeared and whisked her away.

Marty waited for her to call, but two days passed before she surfaced. Rocco was more than happy to keep her company.

# CHAPTER 2

## RECRUITERS GALORE

No matter how dark the forest is,
there is always a path through it.

After a Bruce Springsteen concert, everyone went to Tina Tidwell's crib to party. Tina was a striking beauty with Betty Davis-type eyes and was as wild as a March hare. She, too, had moved from Missouri, so the three of them began to run around together. Stoddard and Marty were thrilled with all the good-looking men. Tina had done well.

Marty introduced herself to a girl lounging on a beanbag chair, Tammy Waterford. Tammy's date was busy doing tequila shots and decided to sit this one out.

"Tammy, do you work in Dallas?" Marty asked curiously.

"I'm a recruiter with Kelly Girl. For a fee, we place applicants in various job positions. The candidate pays nothing. The hiring entity pays our fee, which I split with my employer."

Marty said, "I want to be a stockbroker, but Merrill Lynch turned me down because I've never sold a service."

She explained that all her experience had been in retail. Tammy suggested she come in for an interview and see her office. Marty obliged, and the two discussed how to get Marty what she wanted. Tammy suggested she should get a job as a recruiter, then offered her tips on the process, including avoiding strappy shoes and jewelry, and suggested she wear a navy-blue suit.

Marty immediately began interviewing companies seeking recruiters and received an offer from Personnel Connection. They were touted as the biggest and best in Dallas, so she was thrilled for the opportunity. She left The Tannery West in good standing and began her next chapter.

## THE BUCKSTAFF BATHS
## HOT SPRINGS, ARKANSAS 1979

Stoddard and Marty decided to take the weekend off from their busy cosmopolitan lives in Dallas, so they jumped into her new baby Berlinetta and headed to Arkadelphia, Arkansas.

Their trip was prompted by Stoddard winning the most shots contest…not what she drank but what she sold. While serving as a cocktail waitress at the swankiest nightclub in Dallas, she was quite the competitor when it came to winning money.

Elan had secluded nooks and crannies and Backgammon tables, which provided the perfect surface to do a line of cocaine. Everyone partook. There was no caste system once you entered, as everyone was a card-carrying member. The fee to join was $250 per year, but not for Marty. Stoddard could invite one guest, and Marty was a frequent flier there.

The night of the "shot contest," Stoddard took home an extra Ben Franklin on top of her normal $300. With her tip money, the two girls headed for Arkadelphia. Marty's sister, Mary, and her husband, Gary, lived in a renovated old hotel with their three children, Tina, Timmy, and Trisha. Marty's dad called the crew the Arkansas Indians. They were very energetic, to say it nicely.

The girls purposely arrived late to avoid the rowdy kids. However, when they arrived, the Arkansas Indians were still awake, playing games and watching a recording of Romper Room, a popular television show. The girls joined in and stayed up too late, so the next day they woke up late.

Mary, a perfect homemaker, wife, and mother, had fresh cinnamon rolls, coffee, and plenty of milk. Marty felt that milk should have its own food group because it was so important to her. They had plenty of milk. The kids were hooked, too. Marty was in Heaven.

Marty's younger sister, Lora, lived just south, in the neighboring town of Gurdon, so they planned to visit her and her family. Lora's nickname was LB, short for Lora Beth, and she was married to Doug White. They had one child, Marshall, who was only a couple of months old, but he occupied their every thought.

However, their main target was Hot Springs, with its world-renowned hot springs-fed bathhouses. While discussing the visit with LB, Marty asked about the bathhouses. LB said, "I'm a big fan, but you need to get there early because they quit taking customers at 2 p.m."

The girls headed to Hot Springs in search of the Buckstaff Bathhouse, which Mary highly recommended. They found it funny that it was the only operating bathhouse in "bathhouse row." There were seven total historic bathhouses on the main street, but only The Buckstaff was operating and accepting customers.

They knew they had arrived the moment they saw the bright white building with a large covered porch and blue-and-white awnings. It was frozen in time from the 1920s when the bathhouse first opened. Hot Springs was known as the Vegas of the Heartland because of the gangsters who once hung out there. Marty imagined Al Capone lounging on the veranda smoking a stogie after a treatment in the Bathhouse. It was nostalgic to say the least.

The lobby was like an old train station, with class, its sparsely carpeted floors original to the building. To the left of the check-in counter was the only elevator for the four-story building, which was also original to the building. Marty was immediately concerned that they would enter the elevator and never be able to get off.

Stoddard grabbed Marty's hand upon entering and said, "I think we just entered the Twilight Zone!"

Both girls signed their lives away with the waiver from hell and discussed their concerns with the clerk named Sarah. Marty had to chuckle at her because she looked as old as Abraham's Sarah. In fact, the girls discovered she was really old, as were all the attendants.

The services offered were given to them ala carte, so they configured their day of R&R to include the deluxe experience: bathtub soak in the Hot Springs private Jacuzzi tubs, back scrub, full body shower, sitz bath, wrapped in hot towels, steam box, and ending with a Swedish massage, all for $14.95. Estimated time, four hours.

They paid Sarah, and she gave them a key on a stretchy cord for their locker and guided them to the elevator. Attendant number two must have been Sarah's sister, the same age, and they bore a striking resemblance to each other. Again, Stoddard grabbed Marty's hand, a look of trepidation on her face, wondering what Marty had gotten her into.

Marty figured if all the older people hung out there, it must be more than just a bathhouse. There had to be a connection, and attendant number two explained as they inched up to the third floor on the rickety, old, screechy elevator. "Us old folks came here because these here waters can heal ya."

She told them a story about a man and his affliction, how he had drunk the water from the hot, bubbling springs that poured out in the town center and had been healed of everything.

Attendant number two must have sensed Stoddard's apprehension and tried to relieve her fears by telling her she'd been coming to the Buckstaff for forty years and that she would want to come back again and again after the first experience. She stopped the elevator at the second floor, saying the third floor was reserved for men only and the fourth floor was a lounging area for both men and women.

Attendant number three greeted them, and now Marty was nervous. The attendant looked like Nurse Ratchet from the movie One Flew Over the Cuckoo's Nest. The floor, walls, and ceiling were covered with small white tiles.

Marty looked over at Stoddard and asked, "Are we in a mental hospital?

The attendant led them into the locker room, where they tested their keys and opened their lockers to find big fluffy white robes and scuffs. They took off their street clothes, cowboy boots, and hats, leaving their troubles behind in the lockers. They were dressed and ready for the pampering of their lives.

The locals who were regulars hung their plastic hairnets, scuffs, and soap-on-a-rope on the wall and needed no lockers. Marty wondered what they looked like and decided they were as old as dirt, too.

Their first stop was a giant old claw-foot bathtub with white curtain drapes dividing the tubs. The water was swirling around in the tub, just waiting for them to step in. They could see steam rising from the water, piped directly from the hot springs into the tub. Super deluxe. While Marty and Stoddard were soaking in the whirling water, attendant number three showed up with little sippy cups full of the hot springs water. They almost melted into the bath when attendant number four showed up to scrub their backs.

Marty could hear Stoddard talking to her attendant, and she was enjoying her soak. She was giggling and playing in her tub, so Marty yelled to her, "Do you have a yellow ducky over there?"

Her Attendant rushed into her private tub area with a finger over her lips, whispering, "Silence. No yelling allowed."

Both girls started laughing because they were the only patrons, but oh, the ambience. They soaked for about 10 minutes, then dried off and went to the showers afterward. Marty had seen these showerheads in exclusive homes, but she had never had the chance to experience them. You stepped into the shower and let the showerheads encircle your body with a gentle rain. This was cooler water and felt very refreshing, as if meant to bring them back to life, for they were near comatose by then.

Next stop, the sitz bath. Thinking it was pre-pedicure for her feet, Stoddard stood in it. You can take the girl out of Missouri, but you can't take the Missouri out of the girl. She had never seen a sitz bath before.

Attendant number four chuckled and said, "Sit down! This is for your hoo-hoos!"

The girls knew this term was a nice way of saying your bottom. A hoo-hoo could actually be any body part, but in this case, Stoddard followed Marty's lead and sat down in the small basin whirling with hot water. They roared with laughter and began the sitz bath cleanse.

The attendant led Stoddard to the long stainless-steel tables and asked her, "Where would you like us to wrap hot towels?"

Stoddard responded, "Everywhere. Make me look like a mummy."

"Where do you ache?"

"Everywhere."

She was then wrapped from head to toe with white cotton towels that had been treated with the magical hot springs and laid on the table as if waiting to be carried to her tomb, except this Cleopatra never stopped giggling and talking. The attendants had given up trying to tell them to be quiet. They were still the only guests, so why all the hushing?

Then Marty joined Stoddard and was wrapped where she needed it, on her feet and head. Marty was slightly behind Stoddard's schedule and enjoyed seeing what came next. They laid the warm towels over her, like a blanket, which created a calm cocoon effect, and she drifted off, only to be awakened by Stoddard screaming, "GET ME OUT OF HERE!"

Marty woke up and craned her neck to see Stoddard's head sticking out of what looked like a washing machine; the front cover had been kicked open to expose her naked body. She was in a steamer box and couldn't take the heat. Again, it was one of those unforgettable pictures embedded forever in Marty's grey matter.

Stoddard's neck looked like a giraffe's, craning and hoping to separate itself from its body, which was now on fire. Her hair was wrapped in a white cotton towel from the hot-towel experience, which added to this bathhouse overload. She overbaked herself in the hot towels, then finished with a steam-box cocktail.

All the attendants came running to her rescue. You'd think she had just given birth, for they were all waving their hands and muttering, "Is she all right?"

They all decided she was okay and calmed down. Marty, privy to the whole show and still on her back in hot towels, decided to decline the steam box treatment.

The Einstein of the attendants said, "How about a Swedish massage?"

A Swedish massage sounded perfect. So, the final stage of their session was a 30-minute Swedish massage by Helga herself. All two hundred and fifty pounds of her, which was pure muscle. The attendants all looked like retired Olympians, big boned and ready to rock.

Marty could hear Stoddard chattering away to Helga, then a slap, a swat, and then quiet.

Stoddard had finally either been beaten into submission or was totally relaxed. Marty wasn't sure which one, because she couldn't see her anymore behind the curtains that divided the massage areas. The area was spotless, very quiet, and smelled of Campho-Phenique and Clorox, but in a good way. Reminding Marty of her dentist's office, but without the drilling or pain.

Marty was brave enough to ask a few questions while Helga worked on her backside, all of it, including her glutes.

"What's the difference between a regular massage and a Swedish massage, and why do they call it a Swedish massage?" Marty asked with curiosity.

Helga was not eager to talk, but Marty persisted. "Be sure to work on my cellulite."

Helga slapped her on the place at the top of her legs where Marty pointed to and said, "Honey, that's not cellulite, that's just F-A-T!"

Helga gave her testimony, as some of the other attendants had, saying she had been there for 40 years and had been healed of arthritis by the hot springs, drinking six quarts a day, but she really believed it was the six aspirin a day that did the trick.

Marty and Stoddard met back at their lockers, and both agreed they had gotten their money's worth and then some. They vowed to return someday.

## BACK TO DALLAS

Back in Dallas, Marty walked into Personnel Connection and, on her first day, met the office manager, Bill Levine, and the owners, Dick Green and Bud Garret. Bill gave her an office tour and introduced her to Terry Flannery, who headed up the temporary hiring area. Terry told her they had many temp-to-perm placements that Marty should focus on, since they paid the full commission.

There were fifteen women recruiters in the office housed in the newly built Galleria Mall complex. Personnel Connection was on the second floor of the office tower adjacent to the mall. The location was quite posh, easy for applicants to find, and gave the firm clout.

All the recruiters had cubicles, and Marty's was the first in the room. Her office cubicle was open to everyone, and she loved the attention. The team was quite an impressive crew with years of experience between them. Marty was eager to get to know them all and start making placements. Initially, she would split the commission, but it was a placement nevertheless.

## THE JOB ORDER (JO)

The JO, or job order, was a template-style form that outlined the position's criteria, including title, salary, benefits, and related details. The consultant the employer assigned to the JO assured it included all the benefits to attract the very best applicants. It was the consultant's job to screen and find the top candidate for the position. The employer paid a substantial fee based on the annual salary, so it was essential to accurately list the perks and benefits.

Once the JO was ready, it was distributed to the other consultants to see if they had any qualified people. The faster the consultant got the JO out, the faster the placement. Employers were given a 90-day grace period; if it didn't work out, they received a full refund, and the consultant was charged back the commission. That rarely happened, for the ladies were excellent at matching the perfect applicant for a long-term job tenure.

There was a hierarchy to the positions at Personnel Connection: clerk, CRT operator, receptionist, secretary, and the coveted administrative assistant. Applicants were typically interested in whether advancement was possible, which was usually the case, or at least the consultant indicated it was. The pay ranged from $1,000.00 to $2,500.00 per month.

The consultants were all making big bucks, at least double that of an administrative job. Marty was doing very well, but she had not made it to the top until she landed Arthur Anderson, a Big Eight accounting firm. Mary Portlock, a striking black woman, was the Human Resources Director and required the top applicants. Even clerks were required to have two years of college.

Many big firms hired through Personnel Connection because of their impeccable reputation. They advertised numerous positions in the Dallas Morning News classifieds, resulting in a large pool of applicants. Oil and gas firms, major banks, and real estate investment firms were all calling on Personnel Connection for the best talent.

Each consultant had a clientele. Marty started with zero clients, so her placements were all applicants. Then, she learned how to get a JO. You only needed to call the employer from a classified ad that was not on the protected client list and claim you had the perfect person. Her plan worked, and Marty started making money hand over fist.

Merrill Lynch was looking for a licensed sales assistant. The company was in the same building as Marty's office, so she just walked in and asked to speak to the Human Resources Director or the hiring authority for the sales assistant position. Betty Friedman came waddling out. She was the office manager and hired all the clerical staff. Marty introduced herself and offered her business card.

Marty explained that she had seen the ad for a licensed sales assistant and was curious about the role's requirements and the required license. Betty explained that to be licensed, you had to pass the Series 7 exam, which was quite difficult.

"It is like the bar exam for attorneys," she told Marty.

Her administrative assistants all needed the license so they could take a trade in case their boss was out on the golf course. They both chuckled at the comment, which was partly true.

Betty said, "We use Yolanda Johnson's agency exclusively because they specialize in licensed sales assistants. I believe Yolanda is the only recruiter in Dallas who focuses on this segment."

Marty's mind was buzzing. She planned to contact Yolanda Johnson to get her thoughts on starting as a broker trainee. This could be a big break for Marty, and she intended for Yolanda Johnson to be her new best friend.

She asked Betty for the opportunity to recruit for her, and Betty agreed. Marty thought it couldn't hurt to have another source, and the fees would be competitive if she placed someone.

Betty led Marty into her office, and Marty pulled out her steno pad and began taking notes on the position's salary, the required licenses, and other details. Her mind had already envisioned how to fill this job. She would call Southwest Securities and grab one of their licensed sales assistants. It was common practice to raid a company. That's what recruiters did. Then she would call Southwest Securities back after raiding the place and entice them into joining her ever-increasing client base.

Marty came back to the office and found all the consultants crowded in the break room, staring at the monthly totals. Jackie D'Angelo was first with $14,000. She and Marty were best friends, having formed a bond on their first day together. They called each other "pardner," not partner. It was Texas after all.

Also, everyone wanted to see who was on the $7k list. That meant a Friday lunch at an exclusive restaurant. Marty's favorite was Café Pacific in Highland Park Village, known for its fabulous seafood. Everyone ordered appetizers, entrées, desserts, and lots of martinis. They weren't on a schedule, so the day was over after $7k lunches. It was also a motivator, as the people left behind knew they were missing out.

Each year, the state recruiter association presented awards. Personnel Connection was always in the Top Producers' category. Marty was awarded a Grammy-style trophy for being the third-highest producer in Texas in her second year on the job.

Marty still yearned to be a stockbroker, so she decided to take a two-week vacation and beat the bushes again. This time, she had experience selling a service and could tout her production numbers. She told her office manager, Bill Levine, what she was going to do. He said his sister, Nikki, was a broker in Houston. Marty hoped he would alert her and get an interview with her firm, E.F. Hutton.

# CHAPTER 3

## ENTER THE ROOKIE OF THE YEAR: MS. MARTY BLEDSOE

A day of grief is equal to a year of joy.

Marty accepted the offer with E F Hutton. She was the star rookie in a class of fifty people in the fall of 1986. She earned this award by bagging an elephant, a high-net-worth investor, during her first cold calling session in New York during her three-month training course. She had prepared for the cold calling extravaganza by pulling pages directly from the library's vast collection of business owners. She figured if they owned a business, they had money, and she was right.

Marty didn't land the Hutton position right away. She began a lengthy interview process with Dallas's numerous brokerage houses. These were the traditional wire houses, named after the wire rooms that connected them directly to the New York Stock Exchange.

One manager, Tim Myers, all 5'2"of him, was like Hitler. He founded boutique firms such as Kidder Peabody and Rauscher Pierce. Marty interviewed with whoever would see a woman. The Kidder Peabody interviewer was rude, saying, "I don't hire women because they are too fickle." Marty restrained her laughter by coughing and saying screw you, all in the same breath.

Every interview brought her closer to her target — an offer. She was getting a lot of callbacks, so something was working.

One day, she received a call from a man in Houston who identified himself as Al Hynes of EF Hutton. He said he was interested in speaking with her about a position.

The process wasn't easy. There were seven interviews, weird testing that consisted of one battery exam after another, which tested your senses more than your sales or investment knowledge. One such test required Marty to write every word she could think of in one minute that started with the letter "W." She aced it by filling the page. Whatever was thrown at her, she excelled. Her motivation to get an offer from Hutton was insatiable. Nothing could stand in her way of being a stockbroker, wearing starched shirts, and sitting in boardrooms discussing world dominance or, at least, world-class income.

Marty had always dreamed of sitting at a boardroom table, feeling that such a scenario was the apex of anyone's career. It meant you were upper management, which no woman was a part of unless they were taking shorthand of the minutes for their male bosses.

Men dominated every high-level position. Marty was determined to belong to this elite society because she was a natural-born leader. Maybe because she was on the younger side of a male-dominated family, or maybe because the book, *The Feminine Mystique* by Betty Friedan, was no longer in favor. Women were moving closer to higher education than their mothers, who had sacrificed everything for their families. She wanted more than kids and a husband who provided money for groceries. More than housework and soap operas. She was ambitious and fearless. No man would be her superior. She wanted to be the boss and control the money, especially because she knew she could earn it.

After extensive interviews and discussions, or one might say begging sessions with Al, she was offered the coveted broker-in-training position from the company that had been her primary target all along, EF Hutton.

Al was a shrewd operator, and by hiring Marty, he upped his quota for women. There were only two other women in Marty's office, which consisted of about forty brokers and some old guard ticker tape watchers with large, private, corner offices. Al, however, commanded a tight ship and hierarchy, strutting like a peacock over his domain.

Unbeknownst to Marty, Al had a personal reference from Nikki Levine. Bill, her co-worker at Personal Connection, had called his sister on Marty's behalf. Nikki was in the EF Hutton Houston office, catering to private real estate offerings. Her book was the who's who of Houston socialites. Her backing cinched the offer, and Marty was flown to Houston, where the big dog's office was located, to accept the offer formally.

Twenty-four thousand for her first year, plus bonuses, and three months to study for the Series 7 exam. If she passed, she would join 49 men at the Hutton corporate office in New York for training.

She passed by seven points on the most challenging damn test she had ever taken. She thought, "Thank God, New York here I come."

## NEW YORK, NEW YORK

Marty's first day was spent with the group through Al Hynes's administrative assistant, Kate Penney. Kate was a short, red-headed, blue-eyed Irish girl with a determination to please. She was 100% dedicated to her boss and seemed to perform well in her role as his sergeant-at-arms.

Kate first explained the floor layout and the ordering process. There were the OTC guys wheeling and dealing off their pink sheets of highly speculative stocks. In the wire room, she met Melinda Ray. Melinda was busy inputting orders into her CRT that needed her immediate attention. Orders came first; play came second.

Melinda and Marty became good friends even though their positions were in complete contrast. Melinda was Hispanic and had married a white Anglo-Saxon protestant. She was bilingual. Women used every relevant resource to secure the job they wanted. Good ole' American AND Spanish. She was a shoo-in, not to mention the homemade tamales she randomly brought to the office, which undoubtedly helped some.

She was always willing to take an order. Marty loved Melinda's entrepreneurial spirit. She was a go-getter and didn't mind working hard and fast.

Then came the introductions to the brokers. Sam Ferguson and his secretary occupied a sizable office. Kate said Sam specialized in multimedia equities and limited partnerships and would fly to Hollywood to meet with some of his favorites. Hutton underwrote many deals with Disney through limited partnerships under the name, Touchtone Films.

Sam's advice to Marty was to "Sell the hell out of the Touchtone LPs. Big money for you and bigger money for the client. Good luck, kid."

Next, she met the old guards, Fred Lufkins and Oscar Remington. Their offices were walled off from the pit where Marty's cubicle was located among the other offices. They were considered the big dogs at Hutton, with many secretaries doing their running to the wire room, ticker tape, or break room for frequent coffee deliveries or whatever Lufkins' and Remington's hearts desired. Their assistants appeared to have spent many years running around for their illustrious bosses. In Marty's eyes, they were glorified gophers. She was way past the gopher stage, but now she knew where the real knowledge and expertise was housed, and she intended to set up camp near these gentlemen and their entourage.

She also met two women brokers, Beth Terrana and Elizabeth Wells. Beth's claim to fame was being the cold-calling queen. She would place a mirror before her while dialing for dollars to make sure she looked her best. Marty thought that was very clever and took a mental note of the outcome. She wasn't keen on using a mirror.

Elizabeth Wells was a broker in her late 40s, meticulously dressed. She specialized in 401(k) plans and boasted of managing millions, which afforded her a corner office and great respect. Marty wanted to kiss her feet, but refrained.

Then came the post-rookie area. A pre-rookie had not yet taken the Series 7 exam. The post-rookies had made just enough in commissions over two years to secure a permanent spot and achieve commission-only status. They seemed like childish men wannabes to Marty. High-fiving and chest bumping were common. This was not the environment Marty envisioned for brokers, regardless of their tenure or compensation level. She would never succumb to such tomfoolery. It was beneath her.

It was clear, however, that there was a hierarchy at Hutton—brokers then everyone else. The male brokers in the pit with Marty were a mixed bag. Some were young and aspiring, some were highly aggressive, and some came from the lucky sperm club. Their job was simple—write tickets, lots of them, and then drop them with Melinda in the wire room as fast as they could, demonstrating urgency and a strong commitment to productivity. Basically, commission showmanship. Bravado at its finest.

Kevin Kleinsmith and Eddie Frost took Marty under their experienced wings. They had passed the one-year mark effortlessly by offering IPOs (initial public offerings) underwritten by Hutton. This allowed them to offer shares that were not yet on the market, which could be highly lucrative or a significant disappointment, depending on the offering. The boys couldn't care less as long as they were delivering red herrings and cashing in on the frenzy.

Marty could see a trend developing that she should choose a lane and drive it hard. She wasn't comfortable with anything yet, but she was determined to find the ramp that would get her into a lane.

All new brokers were sent to New York to work directly with the EF Hutton trainers. They had every tool in the investment world at their disposal and used all their wiles to mold next year's rookie class. They were most interested in your ability to call and execute an order from a contact.

Some books were required reading for training, especially those on investment theory and proper business attire. Marty got a big kick out of the Barney's representative explaining the benefits of Armani over Brooks Brothers. She intended to wear both plus Versace. She knew how to dress for success and didn't need a man's suit to prove it.

She preferred a pencil skirt, a Ralph Lauren blazer, and a starched blouse. Even if she wore a ruffly Valentino blouse, it would be starched. Marty's mom spent hours spritzing down Louis Bledsoe's, Victor's, Stan's, and Claude's shirts, then spray-starching them to perfection while watching General Hospital and The Edge of Night. Marty had a deep respect for crisp, sharp white shirts and blouses. She looked the part and never wore strappy slutty shoes. She only wore pumps, usually navy-blue Ferragamo shoes, because they fit her foot like Cinderella's slipper.

Wall Street training was no walk in the park. First, was the New York Stock Exchange, where Marty was positioned alongside the Occidental Petroleum specialist on the Exchange floor. She was fascinated with the opportunity to be there. All the people and money moving around made her head spin.

She took a brief tour of the Exchange's inner workings, showing the DOT (designated order turnaround) computer program, which effectively replaced the specialist on the floor. Years passed, and the daily volume far surpassed human ability.

The rookies sat at the board of governors' boardroom table. Around the giant room were oil paintings of the past governors, all men, of course. Marty heard a small voice within her say, "Is this big enough?" She could not refrain from laughing. This table was as big as a football field, with built-in speakers and microphones. Now, she had a seat at the boardroom table and would recall the experience whenever she needed confidence. In her mind, she had made it.

## THE IPO

EF Hutton's corporate offices were off the beaten path. They were stark gray cubicles that reminded Marty of a prison. She wasn't feeling particularly inspired until she saw the cold calling room. Her heart started racing at the prospect of a large order, which would be her ticket out of the rookie pit and back into an office when she returned to Dallas.

There were lots of introductions and icebreakers. The rookies were starting to relax and enjoy themselves, some way too much. Nightly, back at their hotel, there was a small dingy bar with a piano player. The men were drinking martinis and trading stories about why they were there. Marty was included like one of the guys. Maybe because she was the only woman there, and maybe because they were starting to respect her. It didn't matter. She would be successful with or without them.

Week two of training started with cold calling; everyone's dreaded fate had finally come to greet them. They were told to bring a list of potential clients, so Marty took the Dallas business owners pages she got at the library and started down the list.

Their mission was to secure orders for the upcoming public offering of the Blue-Chip Value Fund, which would trade on the New York Stock Exchange under the symbol BLU. During the IPO, you weren't required to deliver a red herring so that things could proceed quickly without mail delays or objections.

The offering price was $7.00 a share, but that figure didn't really mean anything, for it could go either way. The fund was composed of blue-chip equities and bonds. There were also expectations of dividend income, since most of the stocks in the portfolio paid dividends. This was not a growth fund. To Marty, it was the perfect offering because it was affordable, of blue-chip quality, and brand new to the market. No other brokerage houses were participating in the offering, so EF Hutton had a lockdown on this IPO.

The training room featured long tables with chairs in a classroom setting, and each rookie had their own telephone. In front of the class was another long table with five seasoned Hutton guerrilla-warfare cold-call kings. They had phones, headsets, red buttons, and megaphones. Marty was not intimidated. She found the scene comical. The class gave very little training on what to say to snag a new client, but the goal was to get the prospect to buy one share, especially in the IPO.

Marty decided to start off offering Walt Disney shares, suggesting they would be great gifts for children because of the colorful certificate adorned with Goofy and his pals, and who didn't love Disney? What grandparent could resist the suggestion to buy one share, have it framed, and put the child's name on it under the Uniform Gift to Minors Act?

Her approach worked like a charm. On one of her calls, she spoke with Mr. Walter Hedges, the owner of Dallas Scrap Metals. He had 10 grandkids and never knew what to get them. The Disney shares made so much sense, and he appreciated the suggestion. Marty opened ten new accounts with him.

Mr. Hedges, or Walter, and she were now on a first-name basis. He knew she was in New York working out of the EF Hutton IPO desk, so she told him, "I am working to bring a new fund public, and I have shares you can buy before it hits the market."

She decided she'd better alert the training goons, so she raised her hand. Immediately, she was encircled by the sharks, and one stayed up front on the "listen in" phone. They were mouthing words to her because by this time, she was feeling overwhelmed with excitement. How could this be happening? You call a perfect stranger and extract thousands of dollars just by saying the right words. She was in business heaven.

She gave Walter all the details of the offering, and he asked lots of questions. The training goons coached Marty, and she answered all his questions. What was the symbol? How many shares are offered? What is the anticipated price?

The whole class was now listening with great anticipation.

Walter said in a low, gruff voice, "I'll take twenty thousand."

Marty could hardly speak or contain her excitement. One of her trainers said, "Shares, correct?" in a whisper.

Marty winked and said, "I'll be happy to offer you 20,000 shares."

She almost fainted when Walter said, "Yes."

The trainer was smart to direct her to clarify, because $20,000.00 was a lot less than 20,000 shares. This was her first big sale, and it netted $140,000.00.

She was now guaranteed to be out of the pit back at the home office in Dallas. It was the most significant order any rookie had ever received, and the partying to come was inevitable. Everyone was high-fiving and hopping around like Easter bunnies. There was sure to be a big at-a-girl coming that evening with dirty martinis all around.

The crew ended up next to the old piano in their lobby, singing Frank Sinatra's New York, New York until the lights were turned off, which meant, "Go home, brokers."

## ROADSHOWS

After completing her training in New York, Marty returned to Dallas and entered the offices of EF Hutton, located at 500 Akard Street, 33rd Floor, Dallas, Texas. Marty was assigned to a small, closet-sized office. She was thrilled to be out of the pit with the other rookies, all sitting in their cubicles. Her tiny office was a status symbol, and she planned to climb to the top of the heap no matter how much humble pie she had to eat.

Kate Penney, now the office manager, showed Marty to her new office, explained the protocol for first-year rookies, and said they had to attend every IPO roadshow. This didn't sound like a bad gig to Marty because she had no idea what an IPO roadshow was. She quickly found out when her boss, Al Hynes, announced over their office intercom system, "Attention, all brokers. Massachusetts Financial Services is hosting a roadshow and luncheon at the Fairmont Hotel at 11:30. All rookies must attend."

Marty grabbed her post-rookie friends, Kevin and Eddie, and headed to the posh, iconic downtown hotel for the roadshow. They entered the large banquet room, which was elaborately decorated as if a big party were about to take place. Open bars were in every corner, and the brokers were bellying up to the bars in droves.

Seeing the bars struck Marty as odd, as it was lunch. She was about to learn the two-Martini lunch game. The keyword was pace yourself, according to Kevin and Eddie, who had become big fans of these roadshows. Now, she knew why.

Lunch was an exquisite array of salads, fancy surf-and-turf entrées, and crème brûlée for dessert, plus plenty of alcohol. It was such an elaborate affair, Marty thought Donald Trump might show up.

As lunch came to an end, Marty was halfway through her entrée. Brokers were acting like they'd been raised by wolves, stacking dirty China and burping out loud. Why did they eat so fast? She had been raised to eat like a princess, proper bite-size, chew with your mouth closed, keep one hand on your left leg as much as possible, and, for goodness' sake, no tucking your napkin in your shirt.

Maybe it was the liquor, or maybe it was all the gratis that made the general environment crude, but Marty would not succumb to such unmannerly behavior. She was a lady and now a stockbroker. Her father had trained her well. Louis hadn't been as hard on her as he was on the boys, but manners were to be used without exception in the Bledsoe household.

Then came the IPO presentation from Massachusetts Financial. They presented a boring slideshow that provided an overview of the mutual fund, its objective, and the offering price. They claimed to be the first mutual fund company in the United States, based in Boston, which implied strong experience and money management. Marty was interested.

Back at the office, which was bare bones after the luncheon, things were very quiet. Marty was back in her closet office, reading the IPO material, when Sam Ferguson, the media mogul, surprised her by stopping by. He happened to be in town and was interested in how her first roadshow had gone. Marty thought he was just checking to see if she was drunk, which she was very careful not to be. It was tempting, but beneath her at this point in her career. There were plenty of times in the future to take full advantage of a roadshow, but fortunately, today hadn't been one of them.

Sam wanted to know the fund's objectives: growth, income, or both. He had clients who invested in mutual funds as well, but he had no time for roadshows. Marty thought that someday she, too, would pass up the extraordinary free extravagance of these money-making endeavors.

Marty showed the Massachusetts Financial propaganda to Sam, and Sam said, "There's only one Fidelity Magellan, and no one can compete with it."

Magellan was proprietary to Fidelity Investments and a self-service environment. The manager, Peter Lynch, had made a name for himself among growth fund managers by significantly outperforming their average annual returns.

Marty feared and respected Fidelity. How could she compete? The Mass Financial might work and be her only counter-defense. Massachusetts Financial had, in fact, been the first mutual fund family. The only negative now was the upfront fee of 8 3/4% the investor had to pay to buy the fund. The only reason she would sell the fund was for the commission—she couldn't live on love alone, as her mother used to say.

She was learning that she couldn't believe everything she heard and that she needed to diversify her book of business. In her New York training, she was told the number one issue for clients was trust, and brokers were way down the list of trusted professionals. Stockbrokers ranked above lawyers, but only slightly, so she returned to her basic training—one share of Disney to open the door and then shmooze, shmooze, shmooze.

Marty found that getting prospects to trust a woman was hard. No one ever said as much outright, but the sentiment was clear. If only she could find women clients, she might have a chance at some lucrative relationships.

## THE CRASH

On October 19, 1987, at 3:00 P.M. Central Time, it was the worst one-day selloff in the history of the stock market.

Building her book was very difficult. It seemed everywhere Marty turned, there was an issue. Banks had moved to discount brokerages, Magellan, no-load mutual funds with no upfront fees, and junk bonds.

There was significant interest in high-yield junk bond funds. Marty was deeply concerned about the junk market. She wouldn't touch anything with a high yield in it. Not even a small portion of her client's portfolio could be placed in this asset class. Michael Milken, the junk-bond king, was found guilty of market manipulation. He was basically a slush-fund manager peddling unwanted corporate debt. He was known for his elaborate parties in LA for other money managers. Marty thought it all sounded like a mob boss had taken over, and she wasn't far from wrong.

The markets were in a frenzy over the junk-bond debacle. Rumors on the street were of mergers, acquisitions, and takeovers due to the junk bond market collapse. EF Hutton was not out of the woods. It had succumbed to the junk market, too. Its funds were loaded with high-yielding bonds, most of which were not even rated B or better. The ratings gave investors a gauge of the possible risk of repayment.

On the morning of October 19$^{th,}$ something felt different, and Marty sensed that something was wrong. On the prior Thursday and Friday, the markets were down. The old-guard brokers were mumbling over the ticker tape, looking like zombies.

Marty was asking herself, "What was going on?"

This uneasiness is how it must have felt in 1929 when the stock market crashed. Marty knew the rules were different now, and investors couldn't margin, "borrow against assets" over 80% of their value now. In 1929, it was 100%. RCA went from $500 a share to $5; therefore, everyone was forced to sell it to cover their margin calls, which further drove the market down. She thought, "Surely this couldn't be happening today."

At 8:30 A.M , central time, the market opened with a complete selloff. By noon, the Dow was down 10%. By the end of trading, the Dow sold off 20%.

Everyone was devastated. The news was all bad, and Marty felt like her short stint of eleven months as a broker was over. Still, she believed that when one door closed, a window would surely open somewhere. There was always hope.

# CHAPTER 4

## DISCOUNT BROKERAGE OR FULL SERVICE?

To live in the past is to die in the present.

Hutton was merging with Shearson-Lehman. Marty was very distraught about the marriage as Shearson had a terrible reputation. The company was deep into junk bonds and other highly leveraged investments, which meant Hutton would no longer stand alone as one of the premier wire houses. The new firm would be called Shearson-Lehman-Hutton.

Marty had completed her first full year and was barely at the commission level, just above her $24,000 guarantee. She was still dialing for dollars. That's how she got clients, and she hated it. If only she could work for a bank where money flowed in.

She thought she should reach out to Yolanda Johnson, the personnel consultant who specialized in Series 7 administrative assistants, so she called her and scheduled an interview. They decided to meet at Bennigan's on Park Lane and Central the next day for lunch. Marty had no resume to give her, but felt certain something good would come of the meeting.

The next day, Marty dressed like a banker in a smart suit. After years of counseling and training applicants, she learned what was required to secure an offer. Looks mattered.

Yolanda was running late but seemed excited when she sat down at the table. She had just gotten a call from Shari Waldie, someone she had placed several years ago, and who was now heading up a new office in Lakewood for First Interstate Bank Discount Brokerage and needed a licensed sales assistant.

Marty was offered the position. To her, a discount brokerage meant order-taking and no opportunity to counsel or recommend investments, but she was wrong.

Her boss, Shari, encouraged Marty to recommend investments and gather as many assets as possible. Only the bank's customer list holding Certificates of Deposit (CDs) was off-limits, but walk-ins were free for the taking.

Shari asked Marty to set up meetings with the top five retail mutual funds. These funds were available to all, unlike the behemoths, Fidelity and Vanguard, both of which were self-directed. She called Kemper, Putnam, Keystone, Eaton Vance, and Massachusetts Financial. All firms were eager to see Shari, so Marty got them right in. When they showed up, Marty was included, more for notetaking than anything else, but also to give her knowledge of the mutual fund families.

Ms. Waldie had big plans for Marty. She planned to use her as a full-service broker while she herself visited many bank branches, building relationships with them for referrals to the brokerage.

No incentive was offered other than the prospect of generating fee income, and all branches were interested in that. These fees would help the bottom line even if it meant moving money out of the bank. Shari explained that the money would leave the entire system if they didn't capture assets in-house by giving them options. Money was leaving in droves for self-directed firms, such as Charles Schwab and Fidelity Investments. This plan was a way to keep the assets under the bank's umbrella.

Marty made appointments with all the mutual fund representatives. She had so many questions. She wanted to offer the best available options even in a discount brokerage environment. She planned to set up files to hold brochures, prospectuses, and statistics after meeting with each representative.

She put her first plan into action with Eaton Vance. She really liked the rep, Linda Newkirk, and they became instant friends. These relationships would ultimately determine where Marty would suggest that the bank's clientele place their money. She and Linda had a long training session at Marty's desk in the bank's main floor lobby. There were constant interruptions from the phones, questions from bank customers and employees, and so forth. Somehow, they got through the presentation, and Marty now had a mutual fund family to offer. Next was Kemper.

All the other firms had male reps, and they were all good-looking. Alliance Capital rep, Dusty Holman was excellent at his job, so

Marty decided she would definitely send business his way. He was super handsome, and he knew his stuff. Alliance offered the best fee structure, which sometimes could be a big plus for investors.

Bank customers dropped by frequently to check their stocks, for there was a quote machine in the lobby and one on Marty's desk. She got to know everyone well. A lot of money flowed through the lobby, and more and more of it came to the discount brokerage. Customers appreciated the discount brokerage fees compared with wirehouse fees.

## CALL FROM HELL

"First Interstate Discount Brokerage, Marty Bledsoe."

"This is Al Hynes. You have a contract with E.F. Hutton as a new broker. We are going to sue you for violating the terms. After all the money we invested, we expect to recoup that. You'll be hearing from our attorneys."

Marty ran to Shari and told her what had transpired, but Shari didn't seem bothered. She picked up her phone and called her boss in Houston, Bill Taylor. Shari instructed Marty to wait and assured her that Bill could handle the problem.

Shari explained to Bill what had transpired between Marty and Hutton. Bill was in charge of the discount brokerage and trust departments. She had no idea what kind of influence he had, but she would appreciate anything he could do. This was a terrible situation and could cost Marty her career and thousands of dollars.

Bill called his buddy, Howard Thurman, who ran the trust department in Lakewood, where Marty worked. Bill told Howard, and the two decided to team up against Hutton with an ultimatum. Leave Marty alone, or they would pull all the trust funds from Hutton's institutional money market.

After giving Al Hynes the ultimatum, he chose to drop the lawsuit. That was a big break for Marty. She was free to return to her job, which she loved, without the cold calling. Business began flowing and just kept showing up at her desk.

After what Howard had done for Marty, she decided to give him a visit upstairs in the trust department. He was at his giant wooden desk in a rather ornate office, so Marty gave a tap at his door, and he welcomed her in. She thanked him for what he and Bill had done and explained how important her job was to her. He invited her to meet his small staff, then to lunch with him. Marty thought that was a very kind gesture.

They went to the Grape, a French bistro just off lower Greenville Avenue, and he ordered a bottle of red wine. Marty had a glass or two, but she wasn't going back to the office loaded. The lunch could be a test. Howard drank the whole bottle of wine with no qualms. But he was the boss. Marty thought it was a lot like the two-martini lunch the guys at Hutton were so good at. Howard knew the dance.

Shari had encouraged Marty to go. She was always pushing her out of her comfort zone. Marty was becoming the bank's star, winning over financial service reps and tellers. They were perfect for referrals.

The lunch was interrupted by the manager, Tim Rooney. He introduced himself and told them the best food was at night. He said the chef made specials every night and pointed to the blackboard listing them. He said, "The mushroom soup is to die for, you really should try it."

Marty could hardly breathe. Tim took her breath away with his good looks and friendly smile. He wore a light-blue button-down, exposing his curly blonde chest hair, over khakis and topsiders. "What a cutie," Marty said, dabbing her mouth with a napkin so she wouldn't drool.

Marty grabbed her purse and handed Tim a business card, "I office in the First Interstate lobby, you should drop in and we can do some business."

Looking down at her card, he returned her offer by saying, "I am over there frequently because of our firm's banking relationship."

He shook her hand but kept her hand in his, telling her he looked forward to seeing her again. All that was missing was a kiss. Her heart was fluttering. The hell with stocks and bonds. Meeting Tim was going to be fun.

When Marty returned to the bank, Howard introduced her to one of his employees, Mark Manley. He said to let him know if there was anything she needed from the trust department. He was a good-looking man with black hair and a beard. Marty thought he could be a good ally between the two departments, which later proved to be right. Mark liked to sit in with the mutual fund reps who visited Marty, and before long, they started having lunch together. Mark liked to shop, and they became good friends.

Marty couldn't get her mind off Tim from The Grape restaurant. She had not run into him in the bank yet, so she hatched a plan with Mark to go to dinner there. Marty wanted to see what he looked like at night. Did he wear a suit?

She told Mark everything, so he knew all about her lust for Mr. Tim Rooney. Mark offered a plan, "Why don't we go to the Grape for dinner? I'll pick you up, like we are on a date."

She thought his plan was a great idea.

Marty wore a sleek dress, black nylon hose with the seam up the back, and some sexy slings. Mark wore a smart suit. When they entered the restaurant, Tim was there to greet them. He seated them while staring at Marty's nylons. The intensity between them was apparent.

Tim reached across Marty's chest and dropped the napkin into her lap. He was definitely trying to look down her dress. She wondered if he did that with all the women he came across. Then, he directed them to the blackboard hanging over the pass-through to the kitchen. They could see the chef working away. Tim also suggested they start with their famous mushroom soup and a good Bordeaux.

They both ordered the nightly special, a filet mignon with a bottle of chardonnay, but they started with the famous mushroom soup. Then sorbet. Then their entrée. Neither could eat another bite, so they turned down the dessert tray.

Tim stopped by frequently to check on them, or maybe he was enjoying the view down Marty's dress. He was attentive.

She and Mark split the tab and decided to go across the street to Torelli's for a martini. Mark was commenting on the attention they got at The Grape. He noticed Tim's constant presence and told Marty to latch onto him. What was she waiting for?

## THE PICNIC

Tim was a constant fixture at Marty's desk. He had saved several thousand dollars to invest, so Marty suggested he look at AT&T. She didn't want him to experience too much volatility as a new investor. Plus, AT&T paid a dividend. He was thrilled and wanted to open an account and get started. Marty loved his enthusiasm and the attention it drew. Now, she had a real reason to talk and flirt with him.

He decided AT&T would be his first investment since it had very low volatility and paid a dividend, which is what he wanted. It seemed like a good place to start. Marty had suggested several stocks and asked Tim to research each one. He was learning at a very fast pace.

Every week, he bought more AT&T shares until he had amassed one hundred. He was serious about accumulating wealth as Marty had suggested. She told him it was better to own than to owe. Too many people got caught up in buying expensive cars, condos, and Rolex watches. Their mentality was that if you could afford the payment, you could afford the item. Marty felt that was wrong.

She had given him full-service advice. First Interstate was a discount brokerage, but exceptions could be made. In her mind, anyway.

Tim reached across Marty's desk and took her hand. "Your advice deserves a picnic," he said. "How about I pack up some leftovers from the restaurant, and we go over to White Rock Lake, not far from here, and enjoy the beautiful day?" Marty agreed. She grabbed her purse, and they were on their way.

Tim had already asked Shari if Marty could have the afternoon off, and she had said, "Yes." The coast was clear for an afternoon of just being together and getting to know each other away from business. Away from the stock market and the restaurant. Away from the big city.

The lake was crystal clear and beautiful. Lots of sailboats were on the water, and people were fishing on the shore. Runners and bike riders were making laps around the lake on the pristine trail. Tim knew exactly where he was taking her and had prepared a lavish French-style picnic basket. He even added a red-and-white-checked tablecloth.

Tim asked Marty to go down to the lake while he set things up. He had a large plastic tub filled with goodies. Marty couldn't imagine what was in it, but she was happy that he was a planner. No running by the store, grabbing a bouquet, and giving it to her, and thinking that was enough. She liked everything about Tim.

The scene was set with champagne on ice and real champagne glasses. The spread included cheeses, pastrami, and an array of crackers. Marty was in heaven. There were lots of strawberries and a can of whipped cream. She wondered what the whipped cream was for. Her mind was racing.

She didn't have to wait long; he put the whipped cream in a bowl, took a big, ripe strawberry, and fed it to her. She got some on her upper lip, so he grabbed her chin and pulled her to his mouth, where he licked off the excess. Their lips had never been closer. Then he explained who the host and the boss were, and that Marty was to address him as Timothy if she wanted anything. He explained that they were having sex with food. Marty's heart was pounding.

They clinked their champagne glasses, and then Marty asked Timothy for some cheese. He slowly took a piece of brie and slipped it into her gaping mouth. Then she asked for a cracker, and he obliged. Yes, they were having sex with food, and he was the dominant.

The teasing continued. Timothy took some grapes and slid them into her mouth one by one. He made sure she had eaten the one he had just put in her mouth before he slipped another one in. He was very patient, but his patience was so sexy. A man who could control himself. Not a lecherous, hands-all-over-her kind of man.

He drove a red Jeep. A real one with canvas sides. He was a real man with a real job and real aspirations. And he was totally in control of Marty at that moment. She had worn her workout clothes, which included a small jacket that zipped up the front. Timothy slowly unzipped it down to her navel. Then he kissed her navel. Marty felt faint at this point. There was a zipper on her sports bra, but she felt that he probably wouldn't fool with it out in public, but she was wrong. He only unzipped a little bit of the sports bra to expose her cleavage and then gently kissed her there.

He was all over her, but she realized they were in public and pushed him back onto his pillow. He liked the playful act. He said, "What is my lady's pleasure?"

She replied, "More food. Feed me, Timothy," she demanded.

The sun was setting, so the end of the day was near. Marty had never experienced anything like her time with Tim, and she wished every day could be as special as this. Maybe if they developed a relationship, she would have more days like this.

Timothy took her back to the bank, where her car was parked, and gave her a full-body hug and a kiss. Marty called them movie star kisses. She was hooked.

## SHARI GETS A PROMOTION

Shari told Marty to shut the phones down and come into her office. Marty felt something was terribly wrong. So, Marty set all the phones to forward to the receptionist and went to Shari's office. They had lots of meetings behind closed doors, but this was different. Something was amiss.

Shari told Marty to have a seat. They were going to have a conference call with Bill Taylor, their boss in Houston. Shari didn't look sad, but she surely looked serious. What was this call going to be about? Shari picked up the phone, called the Houston office, and asked for Bill. Apparently, he was waiting for Shari to call because he picked up immediately. Shari put him on speakerphone.

She started by thanking them both for everything they had done and for how much she had enjoyed working there, but she had been offered a job that she could not refuse. George Bush had hired her as his personal assistant. He owned the Texas Rangers baseball team, and she was to be his right arm. His dad was now the President. Of course, she couldn't turn that down! What an opportunity.

Bill congratulated her and said, "Now, what are we gonna do without you?"

She replied, "You have Marty."

"Does that sound good to you, Marty?" Bill asked.

"Absolutely," said Marty.

Now, Marty was the boss of her own domain. She got to hire a secretary, and she became the marketing end of the discount brokerage. She would go to other banks, talk to financial service representatives and tellers, and try to convince them to send referrals to the brokerage. It was a hard pill for them to swallow because they had always been trained to retain assets, even offering competitive CD rates.

Her next focus was the travel club. It was a small elite group of very wealthy bank customers managed by Susie Cox. They would take short trips to museums or the Arboretum, and long trips across the ocean and abroad. She decided to go to Susie to see if they could set up a party for this group. Susie was all in. They would set up the lobby with hors d'oeuvres, champagne, and a bunch of brokerage brochures.

She called Howard Thurman in the trust department to include him in this party. They might as well promote the trust department. The two departments weren't competitors; they were partners. Howard agreed and suggested they call Dan Bittner, who worked at Fidelity Institutional Investments. He said Dan was always ready to back anything the bank wanted financially. He suggested they all go to dinner and get to know each other, so, of course, Marty decided The Grape would be the place to meet. Howard agreed and said he would call Bill Taylor in Houston and have him come up, as well. He thought that Marty had a really good idea and wanted to support it financially.

A date was set for the next week, so Marty had plenty of time to tell Timothy of her plans. She asked the chef to prepare something very special for this elite group. Timothy agreed. The stage was now set.

## THE DINNER

Dan Bittner, the lead representative in the Fidelity Institutional department, arrived first. He wanted to make sure they had plenty of seating and were in a private area where they could all talk without being disturbed. Tim was there to greet him, guide him, and reassure him that they had the best seats in the house. He explained that the chef had prepared a special meal for them, as well.

Little candles and fresh flowers were on each table. The café's walls were painted black, and the overhead lighting was dimmed. It was truly a seductive environment. Perfect for business and monkey business.

The seating arrangement for dinner was at a round table. Dan had purposely put Marty right next to him. Something was definitely going on with him, and it wasn't business. The first time he saw Marty, he did everything but drool. Marty didn't understand how a man could act that way, especially one who was married, but he did. It wasn't Marty's fault she was a knockout.

Marty arrived, and it was just as she suspected with Dan. He was right next to her. Leaning over her and putting his arm around her. She thought that at any moment he might put his hand down her blouse or on her exposed nylons. She made sure not to wear the seam kind. She did everything in her power to give him the message that she wasn't interested, but nothing worked.

Tim took notice. Marty excused herself from the table to go to the restroom. To her pleasure, Tim was in the hallway.

He pushed Marty lightly up against the wall and kissed her. He whispered into her ear, "I'm jealous. I wish I could be that close to you tonight. That old man does not deserve to be sitting next to you, and I will kick his ass if you want me to." They both giggled. He put his hand between her legs, starting with her knees, and slowly caressed her nylons. He got to the garter belt and stopped. He looked at her and said, "Oh, you naughty girl." With him, anything was possible. She planned to be naughty this Christmas instead of nice. He did something to her that she couldn't explain and couldn't control. She wanted more.

Marty had to snap out of it. Timothy had taken over, and she had gone into another world, their world. They had an intense emotional connection, which was also very physical. Then, she remembered she was there for dinner and was supposed to be in the bathroom, so she hurried up and got back to the table. Dan was waiting with open arms.

After six bottles of wine, dinner was over. These men could drink, and they certainly took advantage of the expense account. Marty had learned a lot about Fidelity Investments, but she wasn't that impressed with Dan Bittner. She led him along, though, just like she did the rest of them who fell at her feet.

The next day at Marty's office, a deliveryman showed up with a dozen red roses from guess who, Dan Bittner. The note inside the card read, "Let's play golf sometime. Hugs, Dan." She put the roses on her desk and laughed.

The phone rang, and Marty's secretary said Dan Bittner was on the line. Marty said, "Put him through."

He wanted to make sure she got the delivery, but more than anything, he said he wanted to hear her voice. She thanked him for the flowers and promised that they would play golf together someday. He mentioned that Fidelity was hosting a golf tournament, and she should attend. She agreed. He gave her the particulars, and, of course, the tournament was at a top-notch course.

A couple of pros would be there. Picture taking, food, and a little golf.

Howard Thurman was going to the golf tournament, too, so they rode together. He wanted to hear how it was going with Fidelity and Dan Bittner. Marty said it was going well and that it seemed he really liked her. Howard chuckled. He said, "Yeah, I think he likes you a whole lot." They both laughed.

They returned to the bank and resumed making money for themselves and others. Marty could not stop thinking about Timothy. He had captivated her. He was seducing her, and all she could do was say yes.

Marty's secretary, Kim, came in with an important message from Bill Taylor. All it said was call as soon as possible.

Marty called Bill immediately, and he explained to her that First Interstate Discount Brokerage was being sold to Fidelity Investments. Apparently, someone in the West Coast office had executed a delivery-versus-payment account. That meant the buyer of the stock did not have to pay for it. It was essentially a large margin balance backed by the stock. In this instance, the stock held had reached zero value, leaving the bank out $880,000. Bill said they had 35,000 accounts to sell and that Fidelity had offered a reasonable price, but the employees weren't included in the deal, so Marty was out of a job.

Marty was shocked and scared. What would she do now? She loved the bank environment, or at least the part where people walk up with money to invest. She never wanted to go back to cold calling; she knew that for a fact.

## FIDELITY OR INFIDELITY?

It was time to call in a favor. Her old friend Dan Bittner, even though he was in the institutional department, might be able to help her. She was lucky enough to have his direct line and didn't have to go through the 800 number and contend with thousands of other callers. He had a secretary who answered the phone and wondered who was calling. "Marty Bledsoe," Marty said.

Dan was on the phone within seconds. He had heard about the acquisition and was anxious to hear from Marty. He asked what he could do for her. She explained that she wanted an interview at one of the branches and did not want to be in the call center with everyone fielding calls from the 800 number. Dan said there were only two branches, one in downtown Dallas and one in Las Colinas, which did she prefer? She said downtown.

He said, "Let me see what I can do, and I'll get back to you." Marty gave him her cell phone number.

One thing she didn't want was a relationship with him. He was a married man, and there was no gray area there. She hoped he didn't ask for favors, and he didn't seem like that type of guy. Marty was sure he would do the right thing and would not call on her for the wrong thing.

Dan called the downtown office and spoke with the manager, Mike McClain. He told Mike that Marty was the top producer at

First Interstate, which they were merging with, and that it would be vital for her to be in his office because she might be able to retain some of those assets, given her relationships with many of the customers. Mike was interested. He asked for Marty's phone number and asked Dan if he had Marty's resumé. He said no, but she can provide one. Again, Dan assured him she was Fidelity material. He asked Mike to get back to him after the interview. He wanted to know the results.

Mike quickly reached out to Marty, letting her know he had a position open at the branch he managed in downtown Dallas. He asked if she'd like to come in for an interview.

He said, "Please bring your resumé." She agreed, and they set a time.

Marty left her condo two hours early so she could find a place to park and to make sure she looked like she had just stepped out of a fashion show before the interview. She was pleased to find a parking place very close by that had a meter. She couldn't believe that, in this day and time, there were still parking meters. In fact, she saw a meter maid in action, placing tickets on people's windshields.

The office was on the first floor of a tower, and it looked dark and dingy. It was totally gray with no accent. The front door was right on the street, and it said "Fidelity Investments" on it. She had put Fidelity on a pedestal, but this was not it. She entered the empty lobby to find a big counter greeting her. One of the six reps got up and asked if she needed anything. Marty said, "I have an appointment with Mike McLain."

The rep said, "Wait right here, I'll go get him."

Mike came out of his office into the lobby and shook Marty's hand. Nice handshake, she thought. He was dressed like an IBM executive in a navy-blue pinstripe suit and a light blue button-down. He looked like the perfect example of what she envisioned a Fidelity employee would look like. He guided her towards his office, and they both sat down.

Marty handed him her resumé. He took his time, looked it over, and then started asking her questions.

His number one question was, "Why do you want to work at Fidelity?"

Marty told him about her days at E.F. Hutton when she had to sell against them and how she had always admired their performance. She said she loved everything about Fidelity and felt there was ample opportunity for a woman.

They talked casually about what she had done in the past, who she worked for, and some of her experiences. Mike asked her what her favorite area was, if she had one.

She said, "fixed income. I know that sounds surprising that I am here at a behemoth mutual fund company, but I do love fixed income."

Mike was excited because they were opening the bond desk to branch representatives. They didn't know what to do with their bonds, but felt that they could generate fee income and keep their assets with the firm. They were losing fixed-income assets to competitors.

Mike finished the interview talking about compensation. He was willing to offer her more than she was making at the bank, plus commission. The commission structure was complex and included several tasks that she would be required to perform. Essentially, her role would be to acquire assets and bring them under management.

Mike sat back in his chair and told her he had never offered anybody a job on the spot, but he wanted to do so now. He offered Marty the job, and she accepted. Mike immediately opened his office door and said put the phones down. He gave the reps a minute or two to wind up their calls, and the room was silent.

Mike said, "I just extended an offer to Marty, and she has accepted." The whole crew clapped to welcome a woman. Or maybe not.

He gave her a brief office tour and showed her where her cubicle was located. She was sitting between two men. There were two rows of three reps each, and they were in tall cubicles, again all men. You could hear every word that was said, so there was absolutely no privacy, but Marty didn't care. She was an employee of Fidelity Investments, and that was a longtime dream come true.

Marty felt like running out of the office; she was so excited. She had one thing on her mind: to see Tim. She had to tell him what was going on because she would no longer be able to see him daily. His account had been automatically transferred to Fidelity, but that didn't mean she couldn't assist him anymore. She was in the branch, which meant he would be calling in his trades on an 800 number. Somehow, they had to get around this.

Hoping Tim was there even though it was during the day, she parked in front of The Grape. They were open for lunch, but he was rarely there for that. He basically worked from four to close every day.

Marty opened the door, and he was right there. He knew something was up and just grabbed and hugged her. "What's up, my lady?" he asked. She told him about Fidelity Investments' acquisition of First Interstate Discount Brokerage. He was grinning by now. He knew she'd always wanted to work there, and seeing how she had flirted her way into the position with Dan Bittner, Tim was so thrilled. "My lady deserves a celebration then," he said. Timothy demanded that she return to the restaurant at 5 o'clock and wear her best evening attire.

Marty ran home, flipped through her wardrobe, and found the sexiest black lace dress she could find. She would wear her special hose with the seam up the back. She went out for a manicure and selected a hot red polish. This was going to be a night to remember, she could tell.

Marty arrived at exactly 5 o'clock and went to the door. It was locked. She knocked, and Timothy opened the door. All the tables had been removed except for one right in the middle of the restaurant. There were candles everywhere. He wore a gorgeous navy-blue custom-made suit. She had never seen him look so handsome. He had special jazz music playing in the background. Marty was curious why he was going to such extremes. After all, she had only landed a new job. Did that fact merit a level of celebration like this?

# CHAPTER 5

## MARTY MAY OR MARTY MAY NOT

A mind needs books like a
sword needs a wetstone.

The stage was set for something, but Marty wasn't sure what. The closest they had been was just a kiss. But her heart was tied to his. She was so in love.

Timothy asked for her hand, which she gladly extended. He raised her, grabbed her waist, and pulled her as close as possible. They danced. It was not a ballroom style dance; they moved around in a circle, staring into each other's eyes, anticipating, and wanting each other. He seated her, then served her dinner with all the trimmings. There was a bottle of wine for each serving. Wine for salad. Wine for soup. Wine for the entrée. Then dessert wine. Marty was feeling no pain. She felt like she had left Earth and was somewhere in the stratosphere.

He came to her side and knelt on one knee. He asked her to take a week off between the two jobs. He said, "Would you spend that with me as my wife?"

She was Gobsmacked. "Yes!" she screamed.

They went to the Justice of the Peace the next day and were joined in marriage. Marty had never been happier in her whole life. She finally had a partner whom she could trust and would build a life with. Maybe children will be in their future. They spent the next week culminating the relationship and discovering pure pleasure.

# CHAPTER 6

## THE 800 CALL
## IT WAS TIME TO GET BACK TO WORK

It can't rain forever. The sun will shine again.

The one-week honeymoon period was over, but the honeymoon continued. It never stopped. Timothy was always at her beck and call, and their marriage was a dream. However, she had to return to work.

After several months, it was time to prepare for her annual review with Fidelity. She felt like she was going to have a good review, but you never know with them. Participants had to compete in numerous categories to receive compensation and recognition. Her boss, Mike McClain, called her in for her review. This meeting was either going to be good or bad, but Marty had a good feeling.

"First off, I want to say you had a remarkable quarter, and we are going to compensate you accordingly," said Mike. "You surpassed every goal we set in every category, and this is the first time in the history of Fidelity that a Rep has done this. We're giving you a $10,000 bonus and a free trip to Boston to meet some of the money managers. When you return to the office, you have a new title: Southeastern Regional Fixed-Income Supervisor."

Marty had goosebumps from head to toe. She couldn't believe what she was hearing, and how dare she think that her review would be bad? She had worked really hard and excelled in municipal bonds, but she was open to all fixed-income investments.

Marty had two requests, and they were big ones: First, she wanted to meet Ned Johnson, the owner of Fidelity. The firm was privately held, and he had a daughter whom Marty would love to meet. Second, she wanted to meet Peter Lynch, shake his hand, express her gratitude for the impact his leadership had on her career, and ask for any stock tips he might have.

Mike laughed and said he would see what he could do. "And by the way, there was a ticket for Tim, as well. Have a grand time. You certainly deserve it," said Mike.

They walked out into the office, and everybody was clapping for Marty. Mike told them the news, and they were all thrilled for her or jealous. She wasn't sure which.

Marty and Tim made the reservations to travel to Boston. They wanted to make sure they ate plenty of lobster while they were there. Fidelity had given her an unlimited expense account to use as she pleased. They hoped to see some sights and definitely check out some of the bars. Their hotel was The Four Seasons on Harbor Street, the city's nicest hotel. Marty wondered what their room would look like. She was hoping for a suite.

The porters were buzzing around them like bees when they arrived at the hotel. It was as if she were the Queen of England or someone of great importance. She still hadn't figured out that this trip was a bonus, and Fidelity did it right. The porter whisked their bags away, and a young receptionist guided them into the opulent lobby. The interior featured a lot of dark wood, stained-glass windows, and heavy carpets. The hotel was absolutely beautiful. They walked up to the front desk and were greeted by the front desk manager. She said she had their suite ready, and she would have a porter guide them to it right away.

They all got into the elevator, and the porter pressed the button for the 18th floor, where the penthouse was located. She thought, "Could it possibly be our room?" Yes, it was!

The room had heavy couches, a large dining table, a full kitchen, and a giant, cozy bed. They had a 360-degree view of Boston. In the corner was a fireplace and an open bar. They would definitely be drinking champagne and having caviar.

They settled in by putting on the hotel's big fluffy robes. They felt like royalty. It was a Timothy kind of night. He had packed a suitcase full of toys so he could entertain his little playmate.

There was a knock at the door. It was the porter, holding a stack of pink boxes wrapped in black ribbon. Marty knew from a hundred paces away that they were from Chanel. "Timothy, she said, you shouldn't have." She knew there had to be exotic pieces of lingerie just waiting for her to slip into, and she was right. First, there was a lacy red bra and a G-string with a see-through cover-up. There were five other boxes full of sexy lingerie. She would wear what her master, Tim, directed her to wear. She was obedient to Timothy at this point.

Timothy slipped out of the room for a minute, and she wondered where he was going. When he returned, he looked at her, asked for her hand, and guided her into the bathroom. He had prepared a bubble bath with candles everywhere. He told her to take her clothes off slowly and get into the bathtub. She did what he asked. She felt like she could lick the color right off his skin. So, she stepped down into the tub until her head was sticking out above the bubbles.

Timothy had bought a tray of fresh strawberries and was feeding them to her. He dropped one in her champagne flute. Then he took one and put it in his teeth and made her bite it out of his mouth. He washed her whole body with scented oil, then asked her to step out of the tub so he could dry her. He gently towel-dried her moist body and kissed each shoulder softly, then ran his tongue down her neck.

Next, he asked her to go put on the lacy pink G-string and camisole. She gladly obeyed.

With the bubble bath complete, they moved into the living room, where a lavish array of fresh fruits and cheeses awaited them. Marty noticed a card that she had not seen when they checked in. She thought the porter might have slipped it into the room somehow. As she picked up the card, she noticed how official it looked, with the initials "NJ" on the front. Upon opening the card, she was shocked. Ned Johnson was inviting her to have lunch with him and his daughter the next day in the hotel's dining room. She was awestruck at the thought of having lunch with Ned Johnson, the owner of Fidelity! Absolutely, she would accept.

Timothy was thrilled for her, but he was ready to play. The night was young, and they had yet to experience pleasure.

The next morning, the Porter brought in room service, which included eggs, quiche, fresh fruit, and various juices. They would need the extra food for the night they had just experienced. Marty had to start thinking about what to wear for lunch with the Johnsons. This was a once-in-a-lifetime opportunity. She needed to look good. She chose her cream-colored Chanel suit, a red satin blouse, red pumps, and a black Chanel shoulder bag.

Marty had told Tim he would be on his own since she would be tied up with the luncheon for several hours. Tim thought of Marty being tied up and immediately got a hard-on. Tim didn't mind being on his own. He planned to tour museums, eat scads of seafood, and be a tourist.

The main dining room was a sight for sore eyes. It was bustling with Boston's finest. Marty could only imagine what CEOs, presidents, and other upper-management types were doing there.

She could see Ned and his daughter when she walked in. She recognized his picture from the one in the Fidelity branch where she worked. He reminded her a lot of Charles Stanley, the pastor on channel 13 on Sunday morning. Silver gray hair and a soft blue suit. His daughter was wearing Chanel, too.

When Marty asked the maître d' to seat her with the Johnsons, he said, "Yes, I was expecting you. They've been waiting a few minutes. Would you like me to take your jacket?"

She said no and followed him. Upon approaching the table, Mr. Johnson stood up. He shook her hand, greeted her, and introduced her to his daughter, Melinda. Marty guessed she was in her early twenties and had just graduated from an Ivy League school. She wondered why his daughter was joining them. However, Marty was thrilled that she was, as she wanted to learn more about the personal side of this legendary man.

They ordered lunch and a bottle of wine. Marty wasn't sure whether she should drink, but since Mr. Johnson had ordered it, she felt compelled to partake. Melinda was sitting to her right, so

Marty turned to her and asked all about her role at Fidelity. She wondered whether this legacy would be passed down or used for philanthropy. Melinda was chatty and wanted to know all about Dallas. Marty said she should come down, and she would give her a tour, and that they would visit the stockyards in Fort Worth so she could see some real longhorns.

Mr. Johnson got right to the point. He had to know how Marty was cranking out fixed-income revenue from her branch. Even her region was showing promise. She said, "I simply use the Tom Sawyer approach, telling them to come on over and paint the fence; it's a lot of fun."

She went on to tell him about the many promotions she had created to generate excitement about the bonds in their inventory. She said it was a shame they couldn't coordinate the money market mutual fund managers who bought big blocks of bonds with the branches so they could have some of that inventory.

Mr. Johnson sat back in his chair and said, "Marty, that is an excellent idea. Could you write down your ideas and get back to me on that project? We will call the project fixed income."

Marty felt like she was floating in the air. Here she was with two of the wealthiest people in the world, and you would think they were her cousins. It was like their little secret. They were all of the same mindset and all Republicans. Mr. Johnson even commented on President Reagan and what a wonderful job he had done for their economy.

The lunch was coming to an end, and Marty had enjoyed it so much. She learned a lot about Melinda, and they traded business cards. Mr. Johnson said he enjoyed meeting her. He was quite impressed with her project on fixed income and was looking forward to hearing her suggestions. He mentioned that Peter Lynch would be in his office tomorrow if Marty would like to come by and meet him.

Marty couldn't believe it. She was finally going to meet the iconic Peter Lynch and ask him all her questions. He had built

Fidelity into a powerhouse. This man was someone Marty truly looked up to.

She said she'd love to meet him and asked what time she should show up. He said, "Eleven works." Marty looked at Melinda and asked if she could come by her office tomorrow afternoon after meeting Mr. Lynch. Melinda smiled and said, "Sure." Marty said, "Surely you won't be hard to find, because everyone knows who you are." They both giggled.

Then Marty said, "Mr. Johnson, can I ask you a personal question? "Is it true that you and Charles Schwab made a bet that you couldn't open a brokerage at Fidelity?"

Mr. Johnson laughed and said, "That is indeed true. We were on the top of a mountain in Telluride when we made the bet. Charlie was eager to make the bet, thinking for sure he could beat me, but he didn't." Then, he winked at Marty.

The next day, it was straight up 11 o'clock, and Marty felt like running into Mr. Johnson's office. She could see Peter Lynch through the glass wall. He was taller than she imagined, and she was finally going to meet him. Mr. Johnson waved her in. When she walked in the door of his office, she was expecting herald trumpets or something similar. This was a big moment in her life, and she relished in it.

Mr. Johnson introduced Peter and said he was going to step out for a minute to run some errands, but they could use his office. There were couches over by the windows, but his office was on the 27th floor, and Marty hated heights. She purposely sat with her back to the window, and Peter sat right in front of her. There was a dull silence before they both started talking all at once. Peter started asking, "Where are you from? How long have you been with Fidelity? Are you married? Do you have kids? His questions seemed like rapid fire, but to Marty, just the usual chit-chat.

She quickly got down to business wanting to get inside his head and figure out how he picked all those stocks, so she just asked him outright, "Where do you get your ideas, and how do you make so much money for the company?"

Peter told her a story about his grandmother. She thought such a story was odd, but she listened and hung on every word he said. Marty was with the greatest of all money managers all by herself. He said his grandmother had noticed there were a lot of police cars around the Dunkin' Donuts. She said she thought that it might be a good stock to buy. Peter laughed but said she was right. He checked into it. Dunkin' Donuts' stock was undervalued, and the company was beginning to expand across the United States. He said it was a three-bagger. That meant three times over. He told Marty that was the way to double, triple, and quadruple your money.

That's what the money manager did. They try to find things people use and need and build on that.

"So, your grandmother is the reason you're successful?!"

They both had a good laugh. Peter said, "It's basically just common sense, Marty. But you can never over diversify. That is impossible. Now, do you have any more questions?" Of course, she had many.

Peter let her know that he had a meeting to get to so they finished their talk. Before leaving, he handed her a copy of his new book and autographed it. "Good luck to you, young lady. I have a feeling you're going to rule the world someday."

Marty wanted to scream; she was so happy. Never in her life had she experienced something so wonderful. Fidelity was taking very good care of her, and she had noticed that the company had many women working there. They did not discriminate. In fact, they encouraged women to excel.

Next, she would stop downstairs to see Melinda Johnson and check out her office.

Marty got on the elevator and went to the 17th floor, where Melinda's office was, but when she got off, there were no offices. It was just a sea of cubicles. She noticed above some of the end cubicles signs that said things like 'pharmaceuticals,' 'oil and gas,' 'real estate,' and so forth. There was no receptionist, so she just walked up to one of the cubicles and asked where Melinda Johnson was. The rep acted startled and said she's in the far end on the right. I'll take you to her.

They walked down the long row of cubicles, and people were staring. Marty didn't know what mutual fund group she was in or where all these people thought she was from, but apparently, the name Melinda Johnson meant something significant.

Marty was expecting a giant office with opulent furniture and an open bar.

The rep got to the end of the cubicles, and Melinda was sitting in one of them. She was just a research assistant. Melinda Johnson, who would someday become the owner of Fidelity, was nothing more than a research assistant!

She could tell Marty was in shock, so she pulled up a chair and invited her to sit. She said, "I had to start somewhere."

Then she explained that after graduating from college, she wanted to come learn the business, so her dad put her in the Select Funds group.

The group was at the bottom of the barrel in Marty's eyes, but in reality, it was brilliant, starting where she could earn everyone's respect. Mr. Johnson was a very wise man not to let his daughter just come in and take over, giving her an advantage. He knew how important it was to earn your way, and Melinda was not the type who wanted something just given to her. She wanted to earn her reputation; she was working very hard to do so.

Marty confessed that she was shocked and told her she expected her to be in some gilded office with people running to and fro, getting her whatever she wanted. They both had a big laugh.

Marty was very proud of her as a woman to do what she was doing. She didn't have to start at the bottom, but she wanted to.

Marty left Melinda a few minutes later and went outside to catch the limo back to the hotel, where Tim was waiting.

Tim was eagerly awaiting Marty's return to hear how her big day had been. He was sitting in the lobby, wearing jeans and a pullover. He had been out running most of the day and hadn't showered, but he was so eager to see Marty that all he could think about was her walking through the hotel door.

Marty approached the revolving door and saw Timothy sitting on a couch, sipping a martini. He looked adorable in his casual clothes, but she could certainly imagine what he looked like without them.

He got up from the couch, gave her a big hug, and kissed her on the cheek. "Now, tell me how your day went."

As she began recounting the day's events, he raised his hand to the waiter and ordered a dirty Martini for Marty. Straight up.

When she had finished, he said, "Let's go upstairs,"

They locked hands and strolled out of the lobby towards the elevator to the penthouse. Timothy had some surprises waiting for her. He always had surprises for her.

They walked into the room, and Timothy said he needed to take a shower. Marty said, "I'll join you." They stepped into the luxurious bathroom and used the hotel's finest soap to bathe each other. Marty stepped out of the shower and handed Tim a towel. After drying off, they walked naked into the bedroom. Marty told him to crawl up on the bed because she had a surprise for him.

Marty unpacked some lavender-scented oil she brought from Dallas. She had him lie on his stomach and began working on his feet, then applied it to the rest of his body. She could hear him breathing heavily and asked him to roll over. There was no response; he had passed out. She thought, "Bless his little heart, he must have been worn out from all the running."

The next day, they packed up and headed back to Dallas. It had been quite a trip, one that Marty would not forget. Tim had enjoyed himself and told Marty he would love to return one day and spend time with just the two of them. They promised each other that they would do that.

They arrived at Boston's airport with plenty of time to have a cup of coffee and get settled. Marty absolutely hated running through airports. She wanted no anxiety on this trip. When they returned to Dallas, they planned to hold each other, watch a movie, and have a glass of wine when they got home.

Before boarding, something didn't feel right about her clothing, but she couldn't figure out what it was. Timothy always picked out her lingerie and had done so back at the hotel. She hadn't been paying attention and wasn't sure what she was wearing, but assumed it matched.

They got settled in their seats, and after the plane took off, the stewardesses began going up and down the aisle. They were offered a glass of wine and a meal. Then another glass of wine.

Tim leaned over and said, "I want you to go to the bathroom and take off your top, leave your short skirt on, and everything underneath. I will come join you in a minute or two."

She felt chills run up her spine as she gladly complied and strutted towards the restroom.

Timothy had planned to surprise her the night before with black lace crotchless panties. He had fallen asleep before he could gift them. The next morning, as they were packing, he had laid them out for her along with a really short skirt and her Cole Hahn flats. She loved that he picked out her clothes and lingerie. She hadn't noticed the missing element.

She waited in the bathroom and soon heard a tap on the door. She opened it quietly, hoping it was Timothy. After entering, he lifted her and rested her on the sink. Smiling, he unzipped his pants, lifted her skirt, which revealed the crotchless panties. Making sure she was ready, he entered her, and they made love in the bathroom, joining the Mile High Club.

## BACK TO WORK

After her whirlwind tour of Boston and the Fidelity corporate offices, Marty was absolutely worn out. The thought of going to her cubicle and answering the 800 number weighed on her. She had told Tim on the plane how stressful the job had become.

He said, "Maybe it's time for you to do something else. Even though you've reached the pinnacle of your job and you're making a lot of money, is that what's most important in the world to you?"

Marty had an appointment with her boss, Mike McClain, at 10 o'clock, so she wanted to get her thoughts together before they met. She reviewed her notes from her meetings in Boston, highlighting the introductions to Ned Johnson, his daughter, Melinda, and the famous all-time portfolio manager, Peter Lynch.

She wanted to recap her ideas, but she knew she had to go through Mike first. There was a specific protocol at Fidelity that employees were required to follow; those who did not were ostracized. That's one thing Marty didn't really like. She wished she could be her own boss someday.

Even though the trip was a success and the big project awaited her, she had to tell Mike the truth. She wanted fewer hours and a lighter workload. She was utterly burned out. She didn't know how he would take it, but it had to be said. Marty was not happy in this current environment.

Also, Fidelity had moved its offices from downtown Dallas to Highland Park. It was taking her an hour to an hour and a half to drive to and from the office. Marty absolutely hated the drive in the traffic. It was so stressful.

So, she got her nerve up and walked into Mike's office at 10 o'clock sharp. He was sitting behind his massive desk, looking over statistics. He said one of his big clients was looking for a large block of bonds, and he was scanning the Boston portfolio.

Mike wanted to hear all about the trip, but Marty said she had something she really wanted to get off her chest before they started the review. She told him that she had been driving an hour to an hour and a half to and from work since the move, and the workload when she got there, which amounted to about fifty-six hours a week, was just too much. Was there any way he would consider letting her work around thirty hours?

Mike said, "Unfortunately, I cannot let you go to thirty hours. We don't have any part-time reps here. You'll have to work a full forty hours at least. I understand you're putting in a lot of overtime, so I'll do what I can to lower your workload.

She told him about the fixed-income project she had discussed with Mr. Johnson. He asked her to write up her ideas for the project and get back to him.

She felt better getting things off her chest and was determined to address her job with dignity and maintain her enthusiasm. She had proven herself, which was hard to do at Fidelity, given the size of the workforce she competed against. She just needed to keep her head down and keep doing a good job.

She had already worked out the logistics of the fixed income project by joining Boston and their resources with the branches. Marty was going to give Melinda Johnson a call about a bank of offices she saw outside of Melinda's group that would be a perfect place for the fixed-income desk.

## THE BOND DESK

The problem wasn't that there wasn't enough good inventory in the fixed-income arena, but that there was a bottleneck between the bonds and the branches.

The reps were unaware of what was available for sale. All Marty had to do was figure out how to get ten reps like the ones she used in Boston. When she needed a municipal bond, all she had to do was call Susan Sanders in Boston, and Susan would fax over a list of available issues. So, she called Susan and explained her problem and what she was trying to do. Susan said she'd like to work with her and come up with a solution because she found there was a lot of inventory, as well, and didn't know how to get it out to the branches.

Susan went to her boss and explained what Marty was trying to do and that she had Ned Johnson's blessing. Suddenly, her project was put on the front burner.

Word was spreading fast through Fidelity that they might be looking for a fixed-income manager. Someone to run the desk there in Boston and coordinate the reps with the branches. Someone who could relate to the money managers and entice them to unload their unwanted inventory from their mutual funds.

Marty decided to call Susan Sanders and discuss the position. She felt she would be perfect for the job. She knew how to access the inventory and was excellent at matching clients' needs. If necessary, she would piece an order together, using several different issues, but ultimately getting the required dollar amount. Susan was already in touch with the money managers who were unloading bonds. That's where she got her inventory from, as did all the reps on her floor. She basically needed to tell her boss she knew how to do the job, since she was already doing it.

Susan was quiet on the phone. Marty could tell she was really thinking, but scared. She had nothing to be afraid of except receiving a "no" answer. And worst-case scenario, she'd be back on the bond desk doing exactly what she did every day. Why not get paid big bucks and get a big promotion?

Marty knew just whom to call. Melinda Johnson. If anybody could make this happen for Susan, it was Melinda. They had talked about the office space, and Melinda was well aware of the fixed-income project. Marty had the perfect candidate and office space.

She picked up the phone and called Melinda's direct line. She answered quickly. Marty felt very honored that she would take her call. They had a good friendship, and, as women, they understood what it was like to be passed over by men. Marty told her she felt this was an excellent opportunity for Susan and that she knew she could handle the job because she had done such a good job working through her issues. Marty said that if it hadn't been for Susan, she couldn't have moved the inventory that she did.

Melinda was taking notes from what Marty was telling her, and she knew exactly who Susan Sanders was. She had met her at a cocktail party at Fidelity. She also knew who her boss was and decided to call him. She strongly recommended Susan Sanders for the fixed-income coordinator position. She said she would be very disappointed if Susan wasn't considered.

She called Marty right away and told her what she had done. They had worked together to make this happen, and it was about to become a reality that could change how business was done in the fixed-income department at Fidelity. That was big. Melinda said she was having dinner that night with her dad and would tell him that the fixed-income project was complete. She said she would give Marty full credit.

Marty thanked her for her time and consideration and said they must get together again soon.

"Hello, this is Marty Bledsoe. How may I help you?"

The caller introduced herself as Judy Spademan and said that she was a paid recruiter. "I'm not sure if you can or not, but I'm going to ask. Do you know any reps with discount brokerage, wire house, and mutual fund experience?

"Well, it just so happens I do," said Marty.

A bank in East Texas had retained Judy to find someone to open a brokerage department in a town about 20 minutes east of Mesquite, Texas.

Marty lived in Sunnyvale, which adjoined Mesquite, so she was very interested because her drive to Fidelity was so long.

Marty asked, “How did you find me?”

Judy said, “I guess I just got lucky.”

She wanted to know if Marty had a current resumé. Marty told her she would have it for her the next day. They traded phone numbers. Marty gave her the direct line to her desk, and they promised to speak the next day.

# CHAPTER 7

## THE NATIONAL TEXAS BANK

If you don't like the road you're traveling, pave another one.

What a coincidence that Marty would get a call from a recruiter seeking the exact background she had. She called that a God thing. Marty had been working the 800 number, so there was no way, with thousands of reps at Fidelity, that she would magically end up on Marty's line. She knew this would be a special opportunity and couldn't wait to tell Timothy about it. They were having dinner together that night, so she would let him know the particulars. Bottom line. She had a way to get out of Fidelity.

The next day, Judy contacted her. She had read Marty's résumé and made some comments, "I found some very basic stuff. You misspelled a word or two."

She noticed that Marty had a fantastic career and excelled at everything she did. She had received one promotion after another, plus she had the experience that the bank was looking for. Judy was impressed and felt the bank would be too.

Timothy had bought out the two owners several years ago and taken over the ownership of the Grape restaurant. He was making money hand over fist. He absolutely loved what he did, but there was always time for Marty, his lady. Marty could hardly wait to tell Tim about her good news and the call to Fidelity's 800 toll-free number.

Judy Spademan was now her new best friend. Marty had been a recruiter and knew what it was like to be on the other end. She knew what it took to get someone an offer and get them placed in a job.

Dinner was already on the table when Marty got home. Tim had fixed a fabulous meal and was eager to hear everything Marty had to say. They always jockeyed back and forth about who would make the most money each year. Marty was afraid this year she would lose because she was taking a risk by leaving Fidelity. She was deep in the six-figure range and had beaten Tim in the income race for the last three years. He did not complain, though.

After dinner, Tim thought it would be a good idea to have a mock interview. He would be the bank, and, naturally, Marty would be the applicant. He spanked her on the bottom and said, "Let's get this done."

Tim rapidly fired off a few questions, "Why do you want to work at this bank? What is your motivation? Do you realize we don't have anything for you to work with at this time?"

Marty responded, "You have a trust department, but apparently don't have anyone who knows how to manage money. In fact, there are not too many banks that do."

Marty said, "It's the place for money to go and die. All the trust departments do is pass portfolios around quarterly, with no selling. They have a buy-and-hold mentality."

Tim suggested she not talk about the trust department. They both laughed.

Then, they went into Marty's closet. She had a huge walk-in closet with a built-in cedar closet for her furs and cashmere. All the jackets hung on one rack, and the skirts on another. He suggested a sports coat and a cute skirt. He had no idea some were suits.

Marty said, "Absolutely not. She needed to wear her lucky suit."

It was a light olive-green jacket and a pleated skirt, with a matching silk shirt underneath. She would wear her white pearls and stud earrings. That's all the jewelry she would wear other than her wedding band.

Timothy had their wedding bands inscribed with their wedding vow, "Now to eternity," instead of "Till death do us part." Marty was happy with his selection; she didn't want a big, flashy diamond. She loved the gold band, and it matched all her gold jewelry. She planned to look professional but stunning.

She was ready for the interview and wondered why she hadn't heard from Judy. She decided to call her to see if she could get any information about the holdup. Judy answered right away and told her not to worry. She said, "I know a couple of weeks seems like a long time, but remember, banks move like snails."

She had sent Marty's resumé to National Texas Bank. However, she had not told her the bank's name. Marty just knew it was somewhere east of her.

She also said, "This is a whole new department for them, so they're being very critical as to who they hire."

Her resumé went to John Davidson, an attorney and head of the trust department. He would be the first Marty would have to impress, and then she would interview with both the president and the CEO. They were a father-son duo, Robert and Riter Halsey. The bank had been in business for over 100 years, so they had lots of old money.

Marty promised Judy she would be patient and not look at anything else. That was a ruse, because this opportunity was the only thing she had going for her. She decided to let it go and focus on her job at Fidelity.

Another three long weeks went by before she finally heard from Judy. She had scheduled an interview for the following Monday at 11 A.M with John Davidson. Marty thought to herself, "He must keep banker's hours." To her, all bankers got in at nine and left at three, kind of like brokers on the East Coast. The New York stock market opened at 9:30 Eastern time or 8:30 Central time. Of course, she had to be in her office at 8:30. But banks didn't have to adhere to anything like brokers did.

The stage was set for her to meet John Davidson. She wondered what kind of questions he would ask since he'd never been in a brokerage. The trust department really didn't manage money. They just invested it and held it. She could hear Tim in her head saying, "Don't talk about the trust department." They each felt talking about the trust department might be considered taboo, especially in an interview where she was hoping to land a job. They had agreed that her personal feelings towards that part of the bank should be kept entirely under wraps.

As she set out to do her research, it was hard to get information. The bank didn't have much of a website. They were a small community bank, and all Marty could gather was that they had about $250 million in deposits. They had eight locations, with the main one being in Forney, Texas. The Halseys held all the bank's stock, so it was privately held, meaning there was very little public information available.

She decided to call the bank to get information about their basic accounts. She wanted to learn about their fee structure and what basic accounts they offered. She knew they offered checking, of course, but what were their current CD rates, and did they have any special accounts for seniors? She wondered if they had a travel club for seniors like First Interstate Bank. That's the club Marty wanted to be part of. That's where the real money was.

Marty dialed the number and planned to ask whoever answered about their accounts and CD rates. She was greeted by a live person who said, "National Bank of Texas. This is Kathy Cook. How may I help you?"

Marty almost fell out of her chair when a real person answered the phone. Typically, it was an 800 number where you were instructed to enter one for new accounts, and so forth. Marty thought, "A real live receptionist! How personal, what an exceptional idea."

On the call, she learned they offered National Texas Plus accounts for people 50 years and older. There were no fees, and you were automatically included in their travel club.

Marty asked if she could speak to somebody in the new accounts department. Kathy directed her call straight to the financial services reps. They opened accounts and served as the bank's front end, where all the money came in. Marty told the rep, who introduced herself as Billie Sue, that she was over fifty and asked whether there were any special accounts available for that age group and what benefits they offered. Billie Sue rattled off perk after perk. When Marty asked her about her current CD rates, Billy Sue quoted them.

The big question on Marty's mind was what the facilities looked like. Was it an old, run-down brick building, or a new, stylish bank? She decided to get Tim's help, so she asked him to go to the bank and pretend to open an account. She wanted him to collect as many brochures as possible. He agreed to do so.

He went to the main bank in Forney, walked into the lobby, and noticed the financial service reps were in one area. He walked up to an open desk, and the rep offered him a seat. He began questioning her about all the different accounts they had and told her he was over fifty. He wanted to know everything that he could and asked for a CD rate sheet.

Tim reported back to Marty, saying the receptionist she had mentioned was sitting in the middle of all the offices, out in the open. She was not only answering the phones as if she had consumed three pots of coffee but also handling customers in the lobby.

Marty remembered her old days at Personnel Connection and thought what a steal this would be. She could replace this girl in a heartbeat. He said the bank building was an old red two-story, but the lobby had been refurbished. He said there was an outer bank of offices, and the financial service reps were on the main floor.

All in all, he was very impressed. He said he would like to bank there because of the service they offer. Everyone was so friendly. They might be small, but they were obviously a community bank, where everybody knew everybody.

He said when he walked into First Interstate, nobody said hello or acknowledged his presence, and he certainly didn't know anybody by first name.

He said the people seemed to be all original employees. In other words, there was not much turnover, which was a good sign for Marty.

She decided to canvas as many banks as she could. Asking them about their accounts and CD rates. She tried to diversify the bank sizes by gathering information on both large and small community banks. She also noted whether they had a receptionist. To Marty, having a real person answering the phones was a big deal. Having someone answer the phone was a whole different level of service, bringing a personal touch, because people absolutely hated calling the 800 number and getting no one on the other end. Marty absolutely hated those numbers.

It was important in an interview to do your homework and know as much as you could about your future employer. How did they treat their employees? Are there reasonable working hours? She really had no worries about working there. Based on her research, they were competitive in the products they offered and in their CD rates. She was excited to talk to the bank executives she would be interviewing with about her findings. But she also wanted them to know that their personal touch would help her, and that she could offer something competitive and appealing to their depositors.

The most surprising stat was that none of them offered brokerage services. None of the banks that Marty called offered any alternatives to the typical bank products.

She was in new territory and could build a department that the bank would be very proud of, attracting many, many customers. She could carve out a niche for herself at this small-town bank and bring in plenty of fee income.

The day of her interview finally arrived. She first met with John Davidson and knew that if that went well, she would move on. She had to not only impress him but also let him know she could build this new department. He had her résumé, so he knew she had banking, wirehouse, and mutual fund experience with Fidelity. Marty knew there was no one like her.

Judy had encouraged her to talk about her many accomplishments, but to be ready with a business plan for the bank. It could even be a sketch of how she envisioned the department to be structured.

Marty had gotten busy building a plan. She created a flow chart of employees, financial service reps, and the brokerage. She knew she would need a licensed sales assistant immediately. That would free her up so she could go out and call on the other branches, educating them on how the brokerage worked and how to make a referral. She would suggest a $10 incentive for each person referred. That would come out of her budget, which included salaries and overhead. To become a full-service brokerage in a bank lobby required an extensive conversion. The computer systems had to be linked together with the broker-dealer. The final part of the plan was to hire a broker-dealer to serve as the brokerage's back end. The person would be responsible for crossing the trades, generating statements, and overseeing the brokerage's compliance. This was the key ingredient to the plan, and Marty had found a prospect for the bank to use, which she included in her business plan.

For her interview, she wore her favorite suit, which she and Tim had picked out, but instead of the silk blouse, she chose a white, starched French-cuff blouse. That way, she could wear her beautiful gold cufflinks with her initials. Tim had given them to her on Valentine's Day. She wore her kitten-heel cream-colored pumps and nude nylons. She laughed at herself, thinking it was appropriate to wear pantyhose; this wasn't the time to wear a garter belt. She planned to carry her attaché into the interview instead of a purse. She had several copies of her resume just in case. She had her business plan and her courage.

Why shouldn't she get a job offer? She was perfect for this job. She said to herself, "You are going to get it."

Marty entered the bank and saw the receptionist, Kathy Cook, sitting in the lobby, greeting and directing customers, and waiting on people.

Marty walked up to her and asked where John Davidson officed. Kathy directed her to the elevator and said, "He is on the second floor. Just get off the elevator, then go left. You'll see a sign on the door that says Trust Department."

Marty's heart pounded as she stepped off the elevator and entered the trust department. A secretary was sitting in the middle of the two glass offices. Marty suspected one of them was Mr. Davidson's. The secretary's nameplate read Charlotte. Marty thought to herself that Charlotte probably knew more than anybody in the trust department. She was probably a pivotal part of this bank. She asked to see John Davidson and handed her a business card. Charlotte said that he was expecting her and to have a seat.

John walked out of the office on the left and reached for her hand. They shook hands, and he offered her a seat in his office. Marty offered her resumé, and John said he already had one. He said he would like to know more about her personal background.

Maybe that was his way of starting the interview, but Marty didn't like it. She wanted to get down to business and tell them how they could get rich with a brokerage. She was prepared with her business plan.

The interview continued, and he asked lots of good questions. He commented, "We have been through 125 applicants, so we are not in a hurry, but want to fill this position with the right person. He asked, "Why do you think you are the right person?"

Marty immediately responded, "I feel like there is an excellent opportunity for the bank to capture assets that they would never be able to capture if they did not have a brokerage. For instance, 401(k) rollovers. There were millions of dollars moving in the rollover business as people changed jobs. People really want to work with a single institution, rather than keeping their investments in one place and their bank assets in another. She felt it offered a natural consolidation of the clients' needs. And the obvious benefit for the bank would be the fee income generated."

He seemed interested in how she could generate this fee income. But, before letting her go on, he leaned back in his chair and said, "Most of the people who work at the bank are related. We are big on nepotism."

Marty saw that as both a plus and a minus, but expected it from a small community bank.

She said, "It would be my intention to be friends and coworkers with all levels in the bank. Whether they are related or not."

He then pointed to a picture of his wife on his credenza and said she worked there. Marty thought that was an odd thing to say, but she took the picture as a warning, reading between the lines that everyone talked, so keep things to yourself.

Marty changed the subject by suggesting he look at the business plan she had prepared. He was surprised by this and was eager to see what she had. She laid it out on his big desk and the first page stared up at him with the words, "Hire a Broker-dealer."

This made him curious, "Why wouldn't we just call the trades in, as we do in the trust department?"

She explained, "A full-service brokerage needs access like a lightbulb needs energy. The broker-dealer provides a framework for the entire department because they do all the back-office work. Allowing her to do what she did best, sell."

"I see you've included a licensed sales assistant to be your secretary. Is that correct?" he asked.

"We haven't even talked about a budget, and I'm seeing lots of dollar signs here."

Marty got right to the point and told him she needed about $120,000 to get started. Of course, that did not include her salary.

John said, "I don't get into the money part of a negotiation; that's up to the president. Marty could tell he was having reservations, but she persisted with her plan and was not deterred by his comment.

John then asked, "How would you market the department and where would you get your customers?"

Marty explained, "I'm not proposing to rob the bank. I would do no marketing outside of the bank walls. My sales force would be the financial service reps, mortgage lenders, and tellers. I would ask that the bank offer them a $10 referral fee for every prospect they send my way. I would educate them on what to look for. There are specific signs that identify a good brokerage prospect. For instance, one might ask, "Do you need tax-free investments?"

John was way out of his comfort zone with Marty. Brokerage was so new to him that he didn't even know what questions to ask. He wrapped up the interview and said he appreciated her coming in and all the hard work she had put into preparing. He said to wait to hear from Judy Spademan for any follow-up. He rose and escorted her to the door, which he had left wide open. Marty thanked him and left a little discouraged.

She called Judy as soon as she got home to go over the interview and see if she had heard anything back from John Davidson. Judy asked many questions and wondered whether they brought up the subject of money. Marty told her that she had suggested a budget but had not discussed salary. Judy said it was a good thing because it was really her job. She was the one who had to negotiate to get the big bucks, and she knew what Marty wanted.

If there were a next step, it would be to interview with the president and the CEO, Robert, and his father, Riter Halsey. She noticed that Riter's office was just across from John's, so he had probably seen her. Marty wondered what he thought of her. They both shared the secretary, so Marty was right about Charlotte. She probably knew more about the bank than anybody there. No telling what information she was storing.

Marty was excited to talk to Tim about the interview. She told him about the receptionist, who was beautiful and sweet, just as she had pictured her answering the phone. Tim had been in the bank to see for himself, so he knew what she was talking about. Tim wondered where the interview actually took place. Marty said it was upstairs in the trust department. Apparently, they lumped officers together because the man she interviewed with was also the bank's attorney. She wondered what that meant and what kind of lawsuits they could have, but it didn't really matter. She said he was also in charge of the trust department. Tim made his sad face, and they both laughed.

The phone rang, and it was Judy Spademan. She had excellent news. She said John Davidson was very impressed, and they wondered if Marty could come back for a follow-up the following Friday. Robert and Riter had Rotary Club at noon, so they would both be back in the bank by 1:30. Did that work for her? Judy said it was a very good sign that they responded immediately and wanted her back so quickly. She felt it was clear they planned to move quickly on hiring her. That was good news for Marty.

For the next interview, it was time to pull out the power suit—a sleek black suit, black pumps, and a white starched blouse. Accompanied by her black leather attaché. She would wear no jewelry other than her wedding band. Not even her Rolex watch. She wanted to look the part.

She could feel the energy in the air and knew this was an opportunity to build something great. She sought Tim's advice, which she agreed with 100%.

Marty had given John Davidson all the essential information to make a decision, but she felt the real decision-makers were the Halseys. They owned the bank, and the brokerage was Robert's brainchild. Marty was at ease and ready for any questions they might have. She had a really good feeling about the interview. Something was about to happen to change her life. And it wasn't a baby.

Marty pulled her black Lexus LS400 into the parking lot. She tried not to park too close to other cars so her car wouldn't get damaged. They must be giving away money in there, she thought, for there were so many cars. She walked to the elevator, went to the second floor, walked up to Charlotte's desk, and asked to see the Halseys. Charlotte asked her to have a seat and that she'd be right with her. She was busy fielding calls, and her desk was piled high with paper.

After a few minutes, she came over and said, "The Halseys will see you now."

She directed Marty to Riter Halsey's office. John Davidson's office had a glass front and was just across from Charlotte. Marty wondered what John was thinking, seeing her there with them. She walked into the big, spacious office, and the father-son duo offered her a seat at the desk. Robert was sitting to her left, and Riter was seated behind his desk. There was no nervous energy in the room. It was completely calm, and Marty was sure of herself.

Robert started the conversation by saying, "We are thrilled that you would consider starting a program for us. The bank is moving more towards fee income, and the brokerage could help fulfill that objective. We looked over the business plan you left with John Davidson, and he was very impressed. Why don't we start from the beginning? Do you think a broker-dealer needs to be hired to implement this department?"

Marty assured him, "Yes, the broker-dealer is the foundation of any good brokerage. Coincidentally, I found a small firm in St. Cloud, Minnesota, Primevest, that would be perfect for them. I thought about the major firms like Raymond James and LPL, but I feel like the bank would be a small fish in a big pond."

Robert responded, "Yes, I've heard of Primevest through the Independent Bankers Association of Texas. In fact, they endorsed them into their membership."

Marty was onto something.

"What happens after you hire your broker-dealer?" Robert asked.

Marty smiled and said, "Well, if you hire me, then you will know."

They all laughed, but it was true. All they had to do was hire her, and she would build a department for them. They offered her the job on the spot. They wanted to know her starting salary.

She said it was negotiable following Judy's advice. Judy wanted them to come up with a number, and she would do the negotiating. So, that's what Marty did.

Judy was eager to talk to Marty about the compensation, maybe because her fee was based on Marty's salary. She called and said the bank was open on compensation. They wanted to compete with whatever she had been making before at Fidelity. They didn't want to lose her over money.

"What was your last compensation with Fidelity?" asked Judy.

Marty said it was deep into six figures and to tell them that, but she didn't want to have that kind of compensation. She preferred a base salary plus commission. The commission would be based on fee income she brought in. She proposed a $10,000 signing bonus and an annual salary of $75,000. She added that for anything over $5,000 a month, she would receive 5%. Hence, her incentive was tied to the monthly gross of the entire department.

Marty envisioned hiring more brokers. There was just too much territory, so her compensation would be based on the entire department.

Judy thought all that made a lot of sense and commended Marty for thinking ahead. The commission idea was brilliant. She would have some skin in the game, which always increased commission. She said she would call the bank, provide the parameters, and see how they will respond.

Marty basically already had the job. Now, it was just a matter of figuring out what to pay her to keep her. They knew she was a hot commodity.

John Davidson was anxious to hear how much it would cost to get Marty. He seemed more cautious about the money than Robert and Riter. As the bank's attorney, he might have been more aware of the financials. Marty wasn't sure, but she knew Robert and Riter would make the final decision. They were the visionaries, and they ultimately controlled the whole bank, so it didn't matter what John Davidson thought.

Judy contacted the bank and went straight to the top. She knew John Davidson was her contact, but she asked for Robert Halsey. She got him on the phone, outlined all of Marty's concerns, and explained her compensation.

Robert said, "Extend the offer, and we will pay her what she wants. We need her to start as soon as possible."

Judy said it would probably be a couple of weeks because Marty had to give Fidelity a two-week notice, but she promised to get back to him as soon as possible.

Robert was going to build out an office for Marty in the lobby right across from his. She had told him in her interview that she wanted to be in the lobby with all the financial service reps and tellers. He also prepared an area for her secretary. She would sit right out in front of the office and act on Marty's behalf when she was out of the office.

Marty was so excited to have accepted the job. She felt right at home there, and even though it felt like a step back, it really wasn't. She was finally going to be able to build an entire department from the bottom up at a bank. The right way. She had many industry contacts, so it wouldn't be hard to get it up and running. She would call her old friend, Yolanda Johnson, who specialized in placing licensed sales assistants, and get the search for her secretary underway.

As soon as she gave her notice at Fidelity, they told her she could pack up her things and leave. They didn't want ex-employees hanging around stealing their business, but Marty had carefully selected whom she would take with her. She had not signed a noncompete with Fidelity, so she could take whatever she wanted.

The next step was to secure the broker-dealer, Primevest. Marty called Robert and said she would like to fly to St. Cloud, Minnesota, during her two-week vacation to check out Primevest. He agreed and said he would set up the meeting. He knew a contact there and would arrange a tour of their facility. He wondered how long she wanted to stay. She said that one day was sufficient.

So, the trip was scheduled, and Marty had a notebook full of questions. They had to be able to handle full-service brokerage needs. The only difference she could see between them and a big firm like Raymond James was that she would not be able to participate in underwriting deals, so there would be no IPOs. She thought they looked like the perfect match.

Marty checked into the Fairfield Inn, which was right across the street from the office buildings where Primevest was located. She'd have a continental breakfast and then walk across the street to meet Doreen Johnson, the firm's ambassador. Doreen would spend the day with her, showing her the different departments in the backroom operation and the trading floor.

Doreen was on time, and they were ready to meet Marty. All the department heads stopped what they were doing when Doreen came in to introduce Marty. There was the mutual fund department, unit investment trusts, stocks and bonds, and, lastly, operations. This department occupied the top floor of an office tower that was only four stories high. They were a niche broker-dealer, and their offices proved it. They were not flashy but down-to-earth and perfect to do business with.

The most important part of the tour was the technology department. Marty was eager to see what information would be available to her at her branch. Could she get stock quotes? Could she look at customers' accounts? Could she place trades on her own?

Doreen seated Marty at one of the terminals. She demonstrated how to get stock quotes and set up her computer to monitor what she wanted. She showed her how to input a trade on a mutual fund. They looked at customer accounts and the information displayed. Everything Marty was looking for, they had. Even though they were a small firm, they had state-of-the-art technology. Cutting edge, really. They could compete with Merrill Lynch or any firm on the street, and that's what Marty wanted.

Doreen said they settled the transactions daily through a wire. One wire was sent to the bank, and the bank would send one back for any transactions or deposits. They had streamlined the money flow. Marty asked if they charged any wire fees, and Doreen said they did not.

Brokers in banks were required to be duly employed. In other words, they had to be employed by the bank and the broker-dealer. They would get their paychecks from the bank, but they would basically be employed and monitored by the broker-dealer. That made a lot of sense to Marty because of all of the compliance issues relating to a brokerage. The bank did not know that kind of information. It also protected the bank from litigation if one of the brokerage accounts filed a lawsuit.

They would be required to sign contracts that were renewable annually. Doreen explained that it was pretty expensive to bring on a new bank, and they wanted to make sure they made their money for all the trouble. Marty had no problem with contracts and felt they were actually more lucrative than they should have been. If she were in charge, she would've required a five-year contract.

As the day was winding down, Doreen said they had a conference call scheduled with Robert Halsey. He was eager to hear about the tour. Doreen led Marty into the conference room where the speakerphone was. Robert was excited to hear all the good news because that was all she had. She had done her due diligence, and this firm was perfect for the bank.

They dialed the bank number and were directed to Robert's secretary. She put them right through, saying he was expecting the call. Robert answered immediately and asked how it was going. Marty spoke up and said that they had everything she was looking for and then some. She told him she had the contract and would bring it back with her for him to look over. She was sure John Davidson would want to look at it, as well.

Doreen spoke about the technology and how they had to run it through the bank's computer lines. She said they would send people down to work with the bank's employees and the technology department to get everything set up. Robert said they had several technology experts and that, if they worked with the Primevest team, he was certain they could get the department set up. Then, he mentioned there could be no bank information on any of the terminals. They had to be used strictly for brokerage; everything needed to be kept separate. Doreen assured him that Primevest would not have access to any bank information.

All the questions were asked and answered, and all that remained was to sign a contract and have the technology experts get to work. Robert hung up and thanked everybody for their time. Marty shook Doreen's hand and thanked her for the day. She felt certain they would soon be signing a contract together.

The last step was to check out another bank that used Primevest. Doreen had given her a reference in Harlingen, Texas, Ray Downing. She said he was a top producer, and they moved a lot of money through there. He was bilingual, which was a big plus down in the valley. Marty decided to get on a plane and go down and visit Ray.

Harlingen was a small town, but apparently, it had a lot of money running through it. Ray had a big office and a secretary. That was it. No special signage or indication that this was a brokerage. He was strictly business and seemed irritated by her interruption. He really was a top producer at Primevest, which meant he was probably doing over $100,000 a month in fee income for the bank. Marty wanted to know if there were any issues with the broker-dealer. Ray assured her that they were good at what they did, and she would be happy with them.

There was still the open issue of finding a licensed sales assistant. She called Yolanda Johnson to check in and see if she had found anything, and Yolanda told her about a girl named Jennifer who lived in Seagoville. Marty thought that was great because they actually had a bank there, and it was only 20 minutes to Forney. She wanted to meet her.

An interview was arranged, and Marty met her at a local restaurant. She explained to Jennifer that their offices were being built in Forney at the main bank, so this was the best place to meet. Jennifer had prepared a résumé, and Marty saw it right at the top: Series 7 Administrative Assistant. She was a very good-looking woman and carried herself very well. She seemed like the type who could get things done without being babysat. She was dressed in a cute navy-and-white dress with matching pumps.

Jennifer said, "I'm looking for a position closer to home because I'm driving so far in traffic. I can type 70 words a minute, and take shorthand, if you need me to."

Marty could relate because of all the miles she had traveled working at Fidelity. Closer to home was always better.

They discussed salary: she had been earning $18,000 but would take less to be closer to home.

Marty called Robert on her flip phone, told him she was sitting with a lady who was perfect for the sales assistant position, and asked if she could offer her the job.

"What would the salary be?

"She has been making $18,000."

He said, "You might have just found your sales assistant. Let's give her a try. Offer her the $18,000."

The offices were complete, all the technology was in place, and all the employees were excited and ready for the brokerage to open. Marty had invited the Chamber of Commerce over to have a ribbon-cutting. Lots of the local dignitaries were invited, including the mayor and a lot of the bank's customers. There would be hors d'oeuvres and soft drinks. The stage was finally set for the brokerage to open.

They scheduled the Grand Opening for 3:30, when the bank lobby was usually closed. It wasn't unusual for the bank to do this. At Christmas, they opened up the entire lobby, decorated it, and hosted a huge Christmas party for customers and employees. Marty had invited some of the mutual fund wholesalers to build relationships and secure their help for future parties.

All of the bank's upper management in the Forney branch were also supposed to attend. Marty looked around and saw many of the mortgage lenders, but she didn't see any of the top brass. She wondered why they didn't come and thought their absence was rude. This was a big deal for the bank. It could significantly change their balance sheet.

Marty's secretary, Jennifer, was the perfect little hostess. She was inviting people into Marty's office to see all the technology and to hand out brochures. Marty had brochures prepared by the marketing department, specifically for the brokerage, outlining their many services and advantages. There were plenty of brochures from the mutual fund companies, as well.

Tim wanted to show up and see Marty in her element. He was so proud of her because he had been through the whole thing with her and knew the strife she had gone through at Fidelity. He wondered how she'd be in bed, but he knew the answer to that. Their lovemaking never stopped. They were still on their honeymoon.

With the grand opening behind them, they now had to put an action plan in place. Marty decided to work first on the financial service reps and tellers.

She would teach them the buzzwords a customer might use. She made a chart outlining the brokerage services and how they compared with the banks. She honed in on the municipal bond business because she knew the bank had nothing that offered tax-free income.

Billie Sue led the first meeting and said, "How could they earn referral fees?"

Marty explained, "We will pay $10 for every new account opened based on the referral to the brokerage from any financial service rep or teller. I want to stress, we are a team, we are not in competition, and the brokerage is not here to rob the bank but to build fee income."

Marty told them there was another incentive, and it was a fun one. She said the branch with the most referrals in one month would get a free pizza party. She would call on one of her mutual fund wholesalers to cover the pizza parties and be there to support the brokerage. So, they could get a $10 referral fee and a pizza party. She wondered which branch would win.

She took her roadshow to the other branches and did the same presentation. She was very careful to stress that she was not taking money from the bank, but that the brokerage would be an ancillary service alongside the many services they provided. She told them to think like they had a mini-Merrill Lynch in the bank. Anything Merrill Lynch could do--she could do better.

Robert Halsey's office was right across from Marty's, and he popped in frequently unannounced. He dropped in one day with something on his mind; he looked serious. There were about five other banks in the region whose CEOs were his friends and wanted to learn more about Marty's program. They wanted to understand who Primevest was. Robert asked Marty to check her calendar to see if she was free for a couple of days next week so they could canvass these east Texas banks together.

She was opening accounts left and right and taking in money hand over fist. The program was quite a success. In her first month in production, she did almost $15,000. She got a nice bonus check, but the bank was just skimming the surface. Her assistant, Jennifer, was a big reason for the success. She was positioned in front of Marty's office, but basically right in the lobby. She was pulling people over to the brokerage before they ever got to the bank lobby. She was an absolute gem.

Marty and Robert scheduled visits for the next week. Marty didn't have the heart to tell Robert that it was going to be different in the boonies. Plus, there was only one Marty. But she would do what she could to explain the benefits of having financial services on-site in the branch.

The Independent Bankers Association of Texas had endorsed Primevest, and the small community of banks wanted a piece of this action. The buzzword was fee income. None of these banks had trust departments, so they sent all their business to Robert. Even their 401(k)s were all managed by National Bank of Texas. Again, Marty was very leery that they would be able to set up a program like the one she had. However, her job was not to be discouraging, it was to stand next to Robert and answer questions.

The tours of the East Texas banks had ended, and they were on their way back to Forney in the car, and Marty wondered why Robert had hired her, so she asked him.

He answered by saying, "Because you have the ability."

He told her that he thought she would have a long career with the bank and become part of the family. He said it was very hometown, and everybody knew what everybody else was doing, but that also meant everybody cared for everybody. He was curious if Marty even knew her neighbors. She said she did. She understood what he was saying about the hometown feel because she had already experienced it. The people were so nice and accepting.

Marty was honored that Robert took her on the tour of the East Texas banks. He was showing her off. He knew that what she was building was very special, and they were very lucky to have her. They had a great working relationship and every day grew stronger.

Back in the office, Jennifer had about fifteen messages for Marty. People were calling, wanting to invest money and sit down with her and learn about alternatives. There were 401(k) rollovers to do. Lucent Technology was not far from them, so many of their employees lived nearby. They were starting to lay off people, and she found that most employees had their 401(k) fully invested in Lucent stock. That was so risky. She believed in diversification, not just holding stock in the company where they worked. Her theory was that you date stocks, not marry them. And there was more than one industry, so you should have your money spread around to protect you.

The Forney branch was doing really well because Marty was right in the lobby to handle things, and she had found that the other branches needed someone there, too. It was hard to get bank customers to schedule appointments with her, so she decided to drive to Rockwall to meet them at the bank. She met with the bank's president, Larry Willis. He was an all-business type of guy. There was no small talk about where Marty lived or how she got where she was.

All he cared about was the fee income. He wanted Marty to do the same training class that she did in Forney for the financial service reps and tellers.

The Rockwall bank was surrounded by money. People from Dallas moved to Rockwall to be on Lake Ray Hubbard. It bordered the city, and lots of people lived on the lake. New subdivisions had sprung up everywhere, causing a population boom in Rockwall. Marty was excited to see how receptive the employees would be. They worked so hard to keep competitive rates and keep money in the bank. This would be a real challenge.

Larry invited Marty into his huge office. Everything was new in Rockwall. Quite a change from the old bank in Forney. He wanted to understand how the brokerage worked. What were some of the issues that attracted investors to the brokerage? Would she affect their deposit base?

She explained to him that her job was to look for assets outside of the bank. The only time she had really taken money from a financial services rep's customer was when the customer had too much money for the bank to insure. She explained that they would've lost their deposits if she hadn't found a way to diversify their portfolio. She talked to him about the 401(k) rollovers. She explained they were coming from investments, so they certainly didn't want to roll over into a CD.

The rollover she had done for the lady who worked at Lucent Technologies generated about $3,500 in fee income. The bank would've never seen that income if she had not opened an account for her. She would've gone to another financial advisor in the area, probably Edward Jones. Marty said there were a lot of people being laid off, and a lot of them lived in Rockwall.

Larry moved up in his chair. He was very interested. He wondered how they could get the clients to Marty and suggested maybe they set up a whole day of appointments for her. She thought that would be fabulous. After her training course with the financial service reps, they would know what to look for to help them feel more confident.

A date was set for the training, and Marty called on one of her mutual fund wholesalers to cater in goodies. She wanted to bring Billy Sue with her, since she oversaw the financial service reps in Forney and had been a big help to Marty. She understood what the game was. Her FSR's were bringing in an extra hundred dollars a month from referral fees.

Larry wondered if Marty would consider being in his branch at least one day a week, but she explained that she could not. This brought up the conversation, though, of having a rep in every branch. Marty asked him if he would be interested in that, and he said yes. So, the stage was set for a new hire and a cut down on Marty's driving time. She was spread thin moving around from branch to branch.

She had met a very impressive young lady who worked in the trust department, Jill Slayton. Marty felt they had discriminated against her because she was overweight and wanted to give her a chance. She knew the various types of investments and managed the bank's 401(k). She was perfect for Rockwall. Now, all she had to do was clear it through Robert Halsey.

It was time for Marty's annual review. She had been with the bank for two years and had increased its fee income from zero to $34,000 per month. She managed over 400 accounts. That was way too much for one broker. It was time to review the platform and the program itself.

She met with her boss, John Davidson, and he told her he thought she was doing a fantastic job and that she should keep doing whatever she was doing. It was very short and sweet. She brought up the fee income, and he said yes, that was very good, too. He was like milk toast. Marty did not respect him. He was just an empty suit. She wanted Robert Halsey to be there. He would surely praise her for what she had done and ask about her future plans.

She decided to address Robert in person about what Larry Willis, the president of the Rockwall branch, had talked to her about. He wanted a full-time rep in his branch. He saw the need and bought into the program. This was all good news. The only problem was getting Jill Slayton out of the trust department. Marty had no idea how the trust department would respond. She felt it was a good thing for the brokerage to hire from within. It showed the other employees that there were opportunities. The brokerage department was booming. Her vision was to have a rep in each branch at some point.

She decided to tackle this problem head-on. She made an appointment with Robert Halsey through his secretary. She asked for thirty minutes of his time. She intended to outline a plan for how she saw the department growing. She would let him know about her conversation with Larry Willis and bring up her idea about using Jill Slayton. She felt it was time to hand off some of her workload, and a plan would be needed. She would build up the fee income for each branch, then hire someone to be there full-time.

The meeting was scheduled for when Robert returned from his Rotary Club meeting because Marty noticed he was always in a good mood afterward. The members were his buddies, and he didn't have to be a bank president to be liked.

They were seated at Marty's conference table in her office. She wanted to be on her turf. He was always happy to meet with her and always made time to hear what she had to say. Today's meeting could go one of two ways--he could say no, or he could say yes. Marty hoped that he would say yes.

She explained to him that she was really getting stretched, having to go to all the branches. She said some were doing much better than others, but, of course, the Forney branch was leading the way. Her presence there made a big difference, and she felt like she was missing out on business because she was traveling to the other branches and meeting with so many people. She said her assistant, Jennifer Horn, wasn't at the level needed to make investment recommendations, so Marty had to meet with everyone.

She discussed her review with John Davidson and told Robert she couldn't tell whether she was in good standing. John had appeared vague, and she wanted to know what Robert thought about her performance. Was he happy with what she had done?

Robert put his hand on top of hers and said, "We couldn't do any of this without you."

He wanted to review the statistics on referrals and income flowing to the branches.

Marty had prepared a chart breaking down how many referrals each branch received and the fee income for each branch. Forney was way ahead of the other banks, and Marty explained that's because she was there. She went on to tell him that if they wanted to grow the income in the branches, they needed to put reps in those branches. She let him know about her meeting with Larry Willis at the Rockwall branch and that he asked for a rep.

Robert looked at the statistics that Marty had compiled and stroked his chin. He thought it was very impressive that she had prepared the information, but the most important information was what it said. She was totally right. Forney was beating the other branches by a large margin, and he knew it was because of her presence at the branch. He had seen her in action in the bank lobby, in her office meeting with clients, and fielding hundreds of calls.

She said she would start with Rockwall because they had already requested a rep. She thought that the trust department had the perfect employee, Jill Slayton. Robert sat back in his chair and thought about that. He agreed with Marty and said she could have the job, but she would have to pass the Series 7 exam before she could be moved. Marty agreed.

Marty called Jill in the trust department.

"Hello, Jill, could you stop by my office as soon as possible. I have something important I would like to discuss."

"I'm in the middle of something, but I can come down in about thirty minutes. Does that work for you?"

Marty said, "That would be fine."

The human resources department had provided Marty with Jill's paperwork. She had been with the bank for over ten years, working in the same position in the trust department. Her title was assistant vice president. She saw that she had graduated from Forney High School, was married, and had three kids. Since she lived in Forney, the fifteen-minute drive to Rockwall would be feasible. Marty was eager to hear more about her investment experience.

Jill and Marty were seated at her conference table in her office, so everyone in the lobby could see they were meeting. The rumors would inevitably start, but neither of them was concerned. They were all about the business.

Marty wondered why Jill didn't go on to college, and she told her it was because of the children. She said she got pregnant right out of high school and had to marry, but she was very happy, and she wouldn't have changed a thing.

Jill was eager to tell Marty all about the trust department and her duties. She was basically running the whole department. Marty thought, "She is the trust department."

Marty wondered what John Davidson would have to say about hiring her. His opinion didn't really matter because she had secured Robert's blessing. Jill was intelligent and ambitious, a mother of three children, and a hard worker.

Marty ran through her list of questions. How did she feel about working at another branch, specifically Rockwall? What were her long-term and short-term goals? What was her experience with mutual funds and variable annuities?

Jill answered all the questions to Marty's satisfaction. She was perfect for the position if she could pass the Series 7 test, which was a beast. Jill felt confident that she could pass. Marty told her that if she didn't pass, she couldn't have the job. With that understanding, Marty offered Jill the position in Rockwall, and Jill accepted.

Marty had to excuse herself when, suddenly, she felt nauseated. Robert was out of town, so she ran to his bathroom because it was the closest. She vomited and broke out in a sweat. She wondered what was wrong with her. Was it the Mexican food she had for lunch? Did she have the flu? She came back to the table, and Jill asked if she was okay.

Marty said, "Yes, I think so, that has never happened to me before."

The next morning, Marty couldn't eat breakfast. Tim had made her favorite continental spread with fresh-squeezed orange juice, and for some reason, she was really turned off by everything. Even the smell of the orange juice bothered her.

She told him she'd gotten sick at the bank the day before, but thought it was Mexican food. But this morning she felt different. Tim said they should call Dr. Caddell.

Tim was right, it was time to call the doctor. Something was very wrong, and she couldn't figure out what was causing her condition. She called Dr. Caddell to make an appointment and was told he could see her the following week. She told his nurse that she really couldn't wait a week, that she needed to get in right away.

The nurse said they could squeeze her in that afternoon. When she arrived, they wanted to get a urine sample, so she complied. She had no trouble going to the bathroom these days. She felt like she had to go all the time. She wondered if that might have something to do with the sickness. Finally, Dr. Caddell came in and performed an exam.

He left the exam room, saying he wanted to check something and would be right back. When he returned, he was smiling and said, "I've got good news and better news. You're not sick. You're pregnant!"

Marty told Tim, and the two of them were ecstatic about the news. Tim had secretly put her birth control pills away, and she hadn't noticed. They had been talking about having a baby for two years, but the timing never seemed right because Marty was so busy with her career. She planned to continue working but knew things would be very different. They lived in a huge 6000 square-foot house in Sunnyvale, so they had plenty of room for a nanny and a new baby. Marty's parents said they would come to stay for the first two weeks. Marty needed her mom, who had raised eight kids and knew everything there was to know about a new baby.

When Marty returned to work, she walked into Robert's office and told him the good news. She said it was perfect timing, since she had hired Jill Slayton for the position in Rockwall, pending her passing the exam. She let him know she would send Jill to a one-week prep course and mentor her after she passed the exam.

John Davidson was livid at the news that Marty had hired Jill. Marty couldn't care less; she had done what needed to be done. Business was business, and besides, it gave John an opportunity to put someone in that position who knew how to manage money. But of course, she knew he probably didn't think about it that way, but would worry about how much extra work he was going to have to do.

Marty registered Jill for the Series 7 class, a weeklong cram course. Knowing they had a good pass ratio, Marty thought it was a good idea. She had done it the old-fashioned way at EF Hutton by studying for three months and then taking the test. She knew Jill already had extensive exposure and had probably learned a great deal while in the trust department, handling their 401(k) business. Now that she was pregnant, Marty was depending on Jill not only to pass the test but to do so quickly.

The trust department asked Donna Elder to take Jill's place. She lived in Forney and worked in corporate trust in downtown Dallas. Marty was not impressed with her background. She had no experience handling the kind of trust accounts she would be managing. She probably didn't even know what a mutual fund was. However, it wasn't Marty's problem. She would continue to work with Jill to get her license, then mentor her into a fee-income machine.

Robert had talked to Larry Willis about Jill, told him the plan, and that Marty was pregnant. He told him it would work out well because she would be able to learn from Marty and step in during her absence. He wasn't sure of the time frame, but he told Larry he would move as quickly as possible. He understood how badly he wanted someone in his branch, but he knew it would take time to get the right person, and they wanted to do it right.

Jill passed the Series 7 exam with flying colors. She was now a registered rep and could take trades. Marty made her sit with Jennifer at her desk and learn how to use the computer, how to look up account information, how to place a trade, where to find values for mutual funds, and all the other information that was on the computer.

Marty heard a ruckus in the lobby and looked up to see Donna Elder standing over Jennifer. She wanted to know why Jill wasn't up in the trust department where she was supposed to be training her. Marty walked out of her office and asked if she could be of some assistance. Donna was hopping mad. She wanted to know why Jill wasn't at her desk upstairs. Marty explained to her that she was now an employee of Primevest and reported to Marty and would be spending most of her time in the lobby training. If she had a problem with the situation, she should talk to Robert Halsey.

A battle was brewing between these two women, and Marty planned on winning. She thought to herself, "John Davidson had better step up to the plate and get this woman under control because I'm not going to put up with these shenanigans. Jill is now on my brokerage team. Ms. Elder can find someone else to potty train her." Marty smiled at herself, thinking the situation was almost comical.

The battle took place in Robert's boardroom. Robert had called them all together to straighten out the issues. He began by saying they were implementing a big plan and that they were all team members. Training took place when a manager chose to make it happen. It was up to the specific managers to guide their employees.

Donna Elder said she wouldn't have taken the job if she had known she wouldn't receive any training. She felt misled.

Marty interrupted, "You have experience in trust, so how much training do you need? Jill is now my employee, and she will soon be moving to Rockwall. If you need help, you can have her for one day."

Neither woman liked the other. Donna was intimidated by Marty and felt belittled by what she had said. She didn't want to admit she lacked the right experience. She knew the only reason they brought her on was that she lived in Forney. Marty thought whatever they were paying her was too much. They had given her the title of Bank Vice President, so Marty felt it was up to Donna to figure out a way to succeed. Unfortunately, there was no guidebook for her to follow, and she was absolutely lost. Marty felt like Donna got what she deserved.

After the meeting, Robert told Marty, "I hope we will never get cross with each other, because you are a formidable opponent. I sure don't want to lock horns with you." They both laughed.

Marty decided Jill needed a presence, so she asked her to sit in Marty's office from 8 A.M. to 9 A.M. and from 3 P.M. to 5 P.M., giving Marty the afternoon to visit the other banks and get home early. Her energy was waning, so she knew she needed to slow her pace. She was getting ready to have a baby and needed to start acting like it. The business would always be there.

Tim was always excited to see Marty after a long day. Now he had a baby on the way. He was glad to hear about the cutback in her hours. He believed that assigning Jill to Marty's office chair would provide her with valuable experience and insight into the daily operations.

They began discussing names and trying to figure out what they would do about a nanny. If it were a boy, Marty wanted to name him Timothy Ryan Rooney, and they would call him Ryan. If it were a girl, she would be called Jule Katherine Rooney.

They were starting to look at baby furniture and thinking about colors for the nursery. Since they didn't know if it was a boy or a girl, Marty thought seafoam green would be a good color. The theme would be hot air balloons in pastel pink, blue, and yellow.

Those were all neutral colors for any baby, and they would look so precious in the nursery. Marty planned to have custom sheets and covers made for the crib and changing table.

They really wanted to have a live-in nanny. Marty had heard of a place in Southlake that referred parents to nannies, so she called and asked how the process worked. They explained that they matched the need to the available person. They wondered if Marty wanted a live-in. She said, "Yes," and added that she preferred someone who was no longer in high school. She wanted a mature mother type. She asked about fees, and though they were steep, Marty was determined.

She and Tim set up an appointment at the company's Southlake office to explain their needs. Marty sensed the company was thorough, and it seemed they had a good vetting process to match clients with nannies. They were provided with a contract and brochures. They found them quite impressive. They had not realized a contract was necessary, but were glad because it most likely protected them and the referral company. They seemed to be good business people.

Marty and Tim wanted to know what they were getting into, so they dropped the contract at their attorney's office. They wanted a professional opinion about what they were getting into and any possible liabilities. They waited for him to call back before agreeing to sign anything.

Their lawyer called back and said the contract looked good. Their homeowner's insurance covered a wide range of items. It was essentially a hold-harmless agreement, so they couldn't sue them. They decided to sign the contract, setting the process in motion. The company had told them it might take six months to a year to find a match, but they would do their best to find somebody who coincided with Marty's due date. They said some of their interviews were done over the phone because the girls lived abroad. Several were from Denmark and Sweden. Marty's primary concern was getting a good reference from anyone they recommended. As long as they were good mothers to Marty's baby, she didn't care what country they were from.

Now that things were in place for the baby, Marty could get back to work. She had to focus on Jill. She passed her Series 7 exam and needed training in how the brokerage worked. Marty began scheduling meetings with all the wholesalers to train Jill on the many alternatives they offered. She had a lot to learn in a very short time, so Marty needed to focus on where she could make the bank the most money. She wanted to share with Jill which investments were the most popular based on their performance, especially the variable annuities. American Skandia and John Hancock were Marty's chosen vendors for annuities. The reps were terrific at explaining the benefits and how the product performed overall.

Jennifer was busy watching the phones, so Marty started going through some strategies with Jill. She said it was important to have recurring fees and not lump everything into one investment. Diversification was her friend. She could also offer CDs. If someone needed to insure something over $100,000, they could spread the money across banks across the United States. Marty said it was probably a good idea not to mention that to the financial services reps. It was a last-resort investment because the bank needed the assets in CDs.

Marty decided to replicate the training, so she started a training manual, feeling there would be more reps to come. She didn't want to repeat this training style every time they hired someone. Instead, she wanted a program in place so the reps could go through it on their own. The training program needed to be effective to work.

Jill wouldn't have a secretary or a sales assistant until she reached $20,000 a month in revenue, so she had to learn the operational side. So, Marty felt it was better to get Jennifer involved because she knew the operational side even better than Marty.

Jennifer was the one who sent wires to and from the broker-dealers daily, and that was a big job. The money had to be assorted by account and the exact dollar amounts used.

Next, she assigned Jill to work out portfolios for different scenarios. Marty would describe the investor and their goals, and it was up to Jill to make the recommendation. Then, she started making appointments and taking Jill with her. Jill was instructed to take notes silently and learn.

Jill, from Forney, knew a lot of people, so when Marty had an appointment with someone she knew, Jill made sure to stay quiet. It was easy to get off topic, and that was the last thing Marty wanted to do. She was strictly business, and she had a lot on her plate. No time to waste on chitchat.

Jill was pragmatic and took her time, which was a good thing. Marty didn't want someone running headlong into an appointment and making the client feel rushed.

There were still rumblings from the trust department and Donna Elder. She kept coming to the brokerage, trying to get Jill to help her. Marty was at the boiling point and decided to go straight to Robert. A decision had to be made. It was over for Jill in the trust department, and they needed to make sure that everybody was on the same page. These interruptions had to stop.

Robert was with somebody in his office, or Marty would have just gone in and tapped on the door. She told Donna Elder to go back upstairs to her office and that she would call her later. That was a lie; she had no intention of calling her.

Later, when Robert was free, Marty walked right in. She said, "We have a problem, Houston." Robert started laughing, and Marty was glad, because she was about to lay down the law about Donna Elder. Marty explained that Donna kept coming down and interrupting. She said Jill had spent the day with Donna, as promised, and had trained her in everything she could. Apparently, she needed more training, but it couldn't come from Jill.

Robert said that he would talk to John Davidson and get the problem worked out. He would lay the law down and promised that Donna would not be down in the brokerage again. She could no longer lean on Jill. Robert admired Marty's spunk. There was hardly a day that went by that he didn't tell her she was doing a good job. She had him eating out of her hand, just the way she liked it.

The Wylie branch had been asking Marty to come over to conduct financial services rep training. They wanted to get in on the $10 referral fees, but their bank president, Ken Lane, was a big proponent of fee income. Rockwall wasn't far from Wylie, so there was a possibility that Jill could cover both branches. Marty called Ken Lane and scheduled a training session with his staff. He said he would invite the whole staff. Why train a few people when everyone in the bank needed to provide brokerage referrals, including him.

Ken wanted Marty to work through Marvin Fuller, assistant branch manager. Ken was excellent at delegating. His staff was so loyal to him. He reminded Marty of somebody she went to high school with, so they were going to get along famously. She liked his attitude over the phone, and she would do whatever she could to help his branch. She would even take Jill with her.

Marty spoke with Marvin, and they decided 3:30, after the bank closed, would be the best time for the training. They agreed to have pizza catered in. Marty suggested that the staff bring notebooks because they needed to take extensive notes. She told him she would provide handouts, but they wouldn't learn from those. Marvin said they had plenty of notebooks, and the girls would all be taking notes. He laughed and said he would take notes, too.

The training was scheduled for the following week. Marty had plenty of time to gather brochures and handouts. She wanted them to have enough information so they felt confident referring their customers to the brokerage.

On the day of the training, Marty jumped into her car and drove to Wylie. She had all her propaganda with her and was ready. Jill would be coming too. Marty had told Robert about the meeting, and he said, "Get ready. There's more to come."

It wasn't public knowledge at the time, but they had purchased thirteen banks in East Texas, all within thirty minutes of Forney. Robert thought it was time to ramp up the operation and hire more brokers. They could cover five branches each. Marty said she thought that was a good plan and would start looking for brokers.

She decided to start with the Edward Jones brokers closest to her. They were always unhappy with their setup. Getting to work for a bank where all the money was, would be like finding a pot of gold at the end of the rainbow. She felt it would be easy pickins.

Marty immediately started calling some of the brokers whom she knew in the area. She had crossed paths with them. Most of their clients were bank customers. Marty was in her seventh month of pregnancy and was starting to really feel it. She'd gained only ten pounds, but she felt it in her legs and feet. She planned to hire a broker and get somebody in her office while she was out having the baby.

She called Brad Weddel, who had an Edward Jones office in Mesquite, only ten minutes from Forney, knowing he would be perfect for the job.

He took her call, and she got right to the point, "I'm looking for a broker to service five East Texas banks. Are you interested?"

"I might be, give me some time to think it over. I'll get back to you."

She thanked him for his time and, after hanging up, said a prayer.

Brad called her the next day and said he would be interested in hearing what she had to say. They agreed to meet at the El Chico restaurant near his office. He brought his résumé, which Marty briefly scanned.

"Do you think you can move your client base to the bank?

"I can sure try. If so, I would prefer a tape-to-tape transfer."

That meant he wouldn't have to prepare all new paperwork for his clients, and they would transfer from the previous brokerage firm to the new one overnight.

Marty responded, "I agree, that's the easiest and best way. I'll call Doreen Johnson at Primevest to see if that is possible,

He had done some checking around and found that the National Bank of Texas was building its brokerage daily. He said he kept running into people who had brokerage accounts there, but he couldn't compete. He said he lost a lot of business to the National Bank of Texas, but would not do so anymore. He felt it was better to join them than try to beat them.

"I'd love to join you. I'll be happy to start as soon as I can get my license transferred."

Everything went well with Brad's transfer. His license was clean, with no complaints, and he dressed the part. Marty suspected he bought his clothes at Men's Wearhouse. Those were not JCPenney suits. He trained with her daily at the Forney branch, and it was a little awkward because she was so pregnant. Robert told her she should probably take the last month off, stay home, and eat bonbons. She agreed, and they drafted a plan to make that happen. Tim would be very excited. He didn't want her to work so hard this late in her term.

All the ladies in the bank got together and threw a shower for Marty. She didn't know what half the gifts were for, but she thought she would figure it out after she had the baby. They had a good laugh when she draped a baby blanket over her shoulders as a shawl. They had what she was craving: sheet cake. She couldn't get enough of it. Occasionally, Tim would bring one home, but he was afraid she was gaining too much weight, or he would've given her one every week. Something about the sugar satisfied her. This baby was going to be sweet.

Everything was ready for the baby's arrival. Marty was as big as a house. She could not wait to give birth and lose weight. She was a small girl, but she decided this baby must be huge. They had agreed on names, decorated the nursery, hired a nanny, and made sure Marty's parents were coming down for a couple of weeks after the baby arrived. Marty's mom told her that having a baby was just like an apple falling off a tree. When the baby was "ripe," it would come.

Tim was so excited to be a daddy. Marty knew he would be a good and loving father, maybe even smothering. He was ready for the baby to arrive so they could get back to business in the bedroom. Their playing had ceased since Marty was so big.

Tim had assembled all the furniture they'd bought for the nursery. Basic white. The nursery looked so cute, with seafoam-green walls, pale-pink hot air balloons, and yellow and blue stencils around the top.

The baby was due any day now, and Marty could feel the pressure down her back. She had just awakened from a good night's sleep and felt like she had to go to the bathroom, but couldn't. She sent Tim to Walgreens to pick up some Ex-Lax, thinking she was constipated.

The real reason was that she was having a baby, and the Ex-Lax started the contractions. They called Dr. Caddell right after they realized what they had done, and he told them to start timing the contractions. By four in the afternoon, it was time to go to the hospital.

Marty's bag, packed with all her necessary things, was ready for the hospital. She was taking her own pillow too. She had her fluffy robe, house shoes, and plenty of knee socks. She had heard that it was cold in the hospital to keep it germ-free. The contractions were getting closer. She had finally gone to the bathroom, but she knew now that taking Ex-Lax was not the smartest thing she had ever done.

They arrived at the hospital and checked in through the emergency room just as Dr. Caddell had told them to do. Marty was assigned a room, and before she and Tim could get to it, she was bent over in pain. They put her on the gurney and checked her cervix to see how dilated she was. They determined it was time for the epidural, so they checked for the spot to insert the needle. Marty felt as if an electric bolt had shot up her spine.

The nurses were busy giving her comfort and support. She wanted to stop right there and not have the baby; it was much too painful. But once the epidural was set, she no longer felt pain. The nurses monitored her until her cervix dilated to seven, then they planned to begin the delivery process. Next, they gave her an enema to make sure she was clean before the baby entered the world. Marty thought, “Wow, what a process it is to have a baby.”

When it was time to go to the delivery room, Tim was allowed to be by her side. Marty wasn’t sure he could handle childbirth because there would be a lot of blood and other stuff coming out of her. Not to mention the baby. Dr. Caddell came in, checked her, and said everything looked normal. Soon, he would be telling her when to begin pushing.

What seemed like an eternity to Marty was how slowly this baby was coming out. She wondered whether the timing was normal or if something was wrong. Then, she began to worry, asking herself, “What if there’s a blockage? What if she was having a breech baby?”

She asked to talk to Dr. Caddell.

He assured her everything was normal, “You’re at 10 centimeters, so it’s time to push.”

She was exhausted but told him she would try. Dr. Caddell asked Tim to stand behind her and hold her up from the bed so she could lean over. That helped her push the baby out.

Finally, Dr. Caddell announced, “There’s the head, the baby will be coming out at any minute.”

It was a boy! Timothy Ryan Rooney was born, weighing 7 pounds 5 ½ ounces, at 5:00 AM on March 31st. She and Tim were so happy. The nursing staff took the baby to the nursery, where they cleaned him up to make him all beautiful. Soon they returned with him, all wrapped in swaddling cloth, and laid him in Marty's arms. She thanked God for this tiny miracle, for he truly was a gift from God.

Marty and Tim enjoyed a fabulous filet mignon dinner at the hospital. The hospital prepared a meal for all new mothers, knowing they could finally eat without the terrible gas. They brought baby Ryan in after dinner, and Marty fed him. She planned to breastfeed as long as she could. She figured that when the baby started crawling, it would be a good time to get him on the bottle. Her nanny said she would help her with those decisions.

Marty's parents were traveling from Missouri to Dallas. Ruth insisted they drive because she had so much to bring. No telling what she had in her surprise box. Tim's mom, Kate Rooney, would arrive later in the month. She enjoyed crocheting and said she had made several blankets and outfits for little Ryan. Everyone was happy and started sending presents like crazy. Every day, something new showed up for baby Ryan.

The time had arrived for the nanny to move into their home. They had selected a Hispanic woman who had raised five families. She was in her mid-40s and had a sturdy build. She was tasked with maintaining the house and doing the cooking when Tim couldn't. She did it all. They were paying her handsomely, but she was working full-time, day and night. Her name was Lily Francis. Sometimes she rattled in Spanish, and Marty had no idea what she was saying. Marty frequently reminded her to speak in English.

Baby Ryan was a bundle of joy. He slept 90% of the time, which Marty questioned, "Is that normal?"

She called Dr. Caddell, and he assured her it was normal and that she'd better be glad about it because it wasn't going to be like that for very long. Lily Francis overheard the conversation and just smiled. The Doctor instructed her to wake up every four hours to feed the baby.

Lily Francis comforted her by saying, "We will start using the breast pump to store milk so you can sleep at night. I will help to feed the baby."

Tim was quite a good daddy. He often woke in the middle of the night to feed Ryan and always wanted to be the one to change his diaper. He was a hands-on dad. Marty got a kick out of the breast pump. Tim found it entertaining to watch Marty in action. Her breasts were huge, and she had plenty of milk to go around. She was looking forward to the time when she didn't have to worry about leaking. When her mom was there, she gave Marty a bra with pads, specifically made for nursing mothers. The contraption worked, but Marty was terribly embarrassed. She wasn't sure if she could go through with childbirth again.

Finally, the company had left, and she had only Lily Francis, who was a dream come true. Lily Francis would serve Marty in bed when she wasn't feeling great, and the house was spotless. She taught Marty how to bathe the baby and to use the cotton swabs carefully.

Lily Francis said, "Don't poke him in the ear; babies really don't have earwax, so do not worry."

Baby Ryan was such a joy. He was beginning to laugh, but boy, could he cry. They knew immediately when he wanted something.

Marty got a call from Brad Weddel about a conference with all the major broker-dealers coming up in downtown Dallas, and he thought she might be interested in shopping around. He knew she was a big fan of Primevest, but the market had gotten very competitive. He thought it wise to explore what other state-of-the-art technology might be available. The conference would also help Brad fill the hours necessary for his continuing education program. Marty agreed to go, so they planned to spend the day together. Marty could finally wear her business clothes again, but wasn't sure she could get her feet into pumps. She was determined; after all, she had lost all the baby weight, so she wasn't too worried.

# CHAPTER 8

## BLEDSOE AND ASSOCIATES

What we are born into is not who we are.

The conference was held at the Omni Hotel in downtown Dallas. The big firms planned to be there, like Raymond James, LPL Incorporated, and Bank of America. Most reps came to fulfill their continuing education hour requirements, but people like Marty came to shop for companies. She didn't know exactly what she was shopping for, but felt like she was supposed to be at the conference for a reason. She figured it was a God thing, something that God had ordained and planned for her.

When Marty and Brad arrived, they used the valet service because the Omni Hotel was huge. Marty wasn't keen on walking, since she wasn't quite back in shape after just having a baby. They took the lazy way in. Brad drove a nice Mercedes, so the valet ran to the car and grabbed his key.

Once inside, they realized what a huge conference it was. All the companies had big displays with lots of brochures, and handsome men in custom-made suits. She saw very few women and wondered why. She put the thought out of her mind because she was there to shop, not to get married. She started walking from booth to booth collecting data. Merrill Lynch gave her a free bag, so she began collecting brochures and stuffing them inside.

She asked herself, "What am I looking for?"

She planned to return to the Forney location, where Brad had been working in her absence, and let Robert know she was cutting back her hours but would work from 9 to 3 every day. She felt they might need to hire another broker for Forney because it was extremely busy.

She stopped at the LPL desk and questioned them about their services. They told her they were an independent broker-dealer working with independent advisors. Marty had never heard the term "independent advisor" before.

So, she asked, "How can you be independent?"

The rep explained that they would act as the broker-dealer and that there would be an office of securities jurisdiction (0SJ), managed by a Series 24-licensed person. That person would own the branch and, through a revenue share, receive up to 90% of the broker-dealer's revenue.

"How interesting," Marty thought.

She picked up their brochure, let him know she was local, and they traded business cards. The rep said he'd love to sit down and talk further.

Marty was polite, "I'm only kicking tires. Thank you for your time. I will be in touch if I have any further questions."

She passed from booth to booth and suddenly froze. Under her breath, she murmured, "Drats, it's Primevest!"

She had not expected to see Primevest there. Immediately, she turned and walked in the opposite direction, hoping she wouldn't run into anyone she knew from the corporate office.

She thought to herself, "I have every right to shop around for my bank, so if I run into somebody, so be it, I'm just here to collect information."

The next booth she approached was Raymond James Financial Services. The company had a very impressive background, and all their reps were wearing custom-made suits. They even had women. As she entered their booth, Ray Willis greeted her immediately. He introduced himself as a recruiter looking for independent advisors. He asked for her card and noticed she worked for a bank in a brokerage capacity. He said they have a banking division at Raymond James as well.

"If you would be interested in talking to anybody, I can get a card for you," Ray said.

Marty obliged and said, "Yes, I would like to talk to somebody. I'm keen to learn more about independent advisors and how that works. It never hurts to get more information."

Ray said, "I'll be in town for the weekend. Would you like to join me for breakfast, and I can explain what it is like to be an independent advisor?"

"Absolutely," Marty said without hesitation.

She told him a little about the bank, the assets under management, the number of accounts, and the number of licensed brokers reporting to her. He seemed impressed.

"You have built a good program, but you could do better on your own. You could make three times the commission you are currently making."

That was a statistic they used a lot when people were moving, because they wanted to forecast their future income. He wanted to know if any of those accounts were hers.

Smiling, she said, "Yes, I have over 250 accounts that I personally brought to the bank. My clients are the kind who would follow me to the moon and back. I also manage many of my family's accounts, and I have a very large family."

He informed her that, with that kind of good base, she could hire brokers to work under her, from their homes or wherever they chose, without the expense of a broker-dealer, and that she would be the actual supervisor for other independents.

He went on to say they usually paid a sign-on bonus based on the book's size, which was why he was asking all the questions. He figured she would get a $30,000 to $50,000 sign-on bonus to cover incidentals, since some IRA accounts had transfer fees and some independents liked to reimburse their customers. "Some just keep the bonus for themselves," he said with a wink.

Marty could hardly believe her ears. A sign-on bonus? Her own branch? No more upper management to stop her? No more Donna Elders to deal with?

This sounded too good to be true, and the independent broker concept was a whole new world to her; she intended to investigate it thoroughly. She had the rep's card from LPL and already planned to call him. She felt studying what the two companies offered and how they operated would give her enough information to decide whether to leave the bank and go independent.

Her head was swimming with ideas and concerns, but it was also exciting to think that she could own her own firm. President Marty Bledsoe-Rooney had a nice ring to it.

Back at the bank, Brad Weddle ran into trouble trying to transfer his old customers. Apparently, his noncompete contract stated that all accounts would remain with Edward Jones if he left. He obviously had not done his homework.

He said all he could do was forward his office phone to his cell phone and try to field calls that way. Marty really wasn't concerned about his book; she had hired him specifically to take care of her customers there in Forney. She was more concerned about her book, so the news was good for her. Brad was concerned about his commissions because he would now have to start over.

Marty encouraged him by saying that she would speak with John Davidson, the bank's attorney, to see if he had any ideas. She said it would be nice to have another big client base to add to hers.

She really didn't think there was anything that they could do, and she really didn't want to talk to John Davidson after what happened with Donna Elder; he wasn't a big fan anymore, not that he ever was. Still, she would do as promised for Brad and see whether anything could be done.

Marty received a call from the LPL rep, who was checking in to see whether she had made a decision or had any questions. She told him, "I don't plan to be there much longer, so I'm not interested in moving the bank's business to LPL. However, I am interested in talking to the department that recruits independent advisors."

He was surprised to hear that. She swore him to secrecy, and he promised to get the recruiters to call her and explain their program.

"I'm curious, why would you be reluctant to move the bank's business?"

"They don't want to make a change; they are happy with their broker-dealer network. As you probably know, banks don't handle change well anyway."

She called John Davidson to ask whether he was available to meet. She wanted to discuss Brad Weddel's book of business and preferred that no one at the bank know about their meeting. He agreed and invited her up to the office. When she entered, he closed the curtains on his glass wall. She explained Brad's situation and asked whether there was anything he could do.

He said, "Yes, I will give them a call. Since Brad is duly employed, I will rely on the bank side of his employment to help relieve the contractual restraint."

In the meantime, Marty had a plan. She would call Ray Willis at Raymond James to schedule a conference call since he was in Tampa, Florida, at the Raymond James corporate office. She had many questions, and it was time to get down to the nitty-gritty and understand what an independent advisor meant and stood for. What were her boundaries? Did she have any boundaries? Did they have any leads on independents who wanted supervision? In other words, they didn't want to be completely independent. Especially if they didn't have a Series 24 license, they would need a supervisor, period.

Marty called, and the woman who answered said Ray would get back to her on her cell phone right away. She decided it would be best to leave the bank and wait for his call at a nearby diner. She didn't want anyone from the bank to overhear what they would be discussing. When Ray called, Marty asked her questions, and he answered to her satisfaction. She asked to see the contract they wanted her to sign, and he said he would mail one out immediately, then asked for her home address. She wanted to review it with Tim, then have her attorney look it over.

This was a huge step for her, and she didn't want it to be in the wrong direction. Most importantly, she did not want to violate the noncompete that she had signed with the bank. There was a radius clause in the noncompete, and her office would be far enough away. She was interested only in the clients she brought to the bank. She was not interested in taking the referrals that she had made while working at the bank.

Jennifer buzzed Marty to say she had a call on hold from Heidi Becker. Marty had never heard of her, but she took the call. Heidi was with another bank that had a brokerage, and was wondering if Marty was hiring. She was with a competitor, so Marty asked if she could bring any accounts with her, and she said, "Absolutely." She said that she had worked at an Edward Jones branch as an extra broker before coming to the bank, so she had her own clientele, but she could definitely pull some from the bank, as well.

They made an appointment to meet the next day in Rockwall, which was about an equal drive for both of them. Marty had asked her to bring her resumé, which Heidi had prepared. They had spoken over the phone, and Marty detected a German accent. Heidi had moved to the United States when she was eighteen, so she still carried a German accent. Her diction was perfect, though.

Marty decided not to talk to Heidi about the bank. She would give her a rough overview of how they were doing, but she would recruit her for her own office. If she signed the paperwork with Raymond James, she would have her own branch, and Heidi could work out of her own branch and earn up to 40%. The normal payout for a branch employee at the bank was 3%. This was a huge increase and quite an incentive for Heidi to consider.

The two women met for lunch the next day and got along famously. They were about the same age, but Heidi had that wonderful German accent. It made her very unique, and Marty felt her clients probably loved her. Marty wondered if she had a non-compete. Heidi said she did not. The bank she worked for wasn't very savvy. But no, she had no ties to that bank.

Marty explained that she had been talking with Raymond James about opening her own branch, an office of securities jurisdiction (OSJ). She said if she had her own branch, Heidi could work wherever she wanted to and be her own boss, but that she would be monitored and audited by Marty annually. Her errors-and-omissions insurance would be paid automatically. That insurance was needed in case there was a trading error, and the firm would be covered for any loss up to $30,000.This insurance was required for all brokers.

Marty said she had been invited to go to their corporate offices in Tampa. She wondered if Heidi would go with her. She said two heads are better than one. She was sure that Raymond James would pay for her as well. So, the ladies planned a trip and got ready to ask a lot of questions. There was a lot to learn and a lot to know.

Marty called Ray Willis, "I have another broker coming along for the tour of the corporate offices in Tampa. Are you okay with that?"

"Absolutely, she is welcome." Ray was happy to have any brokers Marty could bring.

He inquired about her name for her badge. They had tight security at the corporate offices, and everyone had to be cleared.

"Heidi Becker," Marty said proudly and added, "She is an experienced broker."

"Tom James, the son of Raymond James, works here, and I've asked him to show you around. He suggested showing you the family's private art collection. Please get in touch with my secretary, and she will make all the arrangements for you and Heidi."

He indicated that they would cover all expenses, including daily per diem.

She and Heidi got on the speakerphone and called Ray's secretary to make plans for their trip. She was quite cordial and accommodating, saying, "I will take good care of you and will secure the best flights and book rooms in a nice hotel which is close by. Would you prefer to travel in the morning or the afternoon?"

They both decided that arriving the afternoon before their tour was scheduled would be best. That way, they could get a good night's rest before meeting with Ray.

"Great, I will handle all the details and overnight the tickets to you. Since you will be arriving on Saturday, you won't have to worry about traffic; this place will be a ghost town."

Marty did not want the bank to know what she was up to. It would be a quick trip to Tampa and back, but she planned to return with contracts. Marty was really looking forward to the tour. She would be the one asking questions, and she had a mountain of them. Marty suggested to Heidi that it would be best for her to do all the talking and for Heidi to listen and provide support.

They both decided to dress semi-professionally in pantsuits. It would be much more comfortable on the plane, and they could wear flats instead of high heels. They imagined that they would be doing a lot of walking, and flats would be much more comfortable.

Ray greeted them at the reception desk and immediately took them up a flight of stairs to the executive level. Everything was glass, except for the white interior walls, which were covered with massive pieces of artwork. Tom James was a world-renowned art collector and kept most of his art at the Raymond James corporate office.

There were many introductions and many questions. Marty couldn't wait to see the fixed-income trading floor. It had been a long time since she had witnessed bond traders, and she was most excited to see what their inventory looked like.

She handed Ray the list of people she wanted to meet, and fixed income was at the top. She wanted to see the mutual fund department, variable and fixed annuities, stock trading, operations, and the insurance department. She also wanted to spend time in the compliance department.

Ray looked over her list and said, "I think you will be impressed. I've planned for us to stop by each of these areas and then some and have made special arrangements so the two of you can meet most of the staff."

They entered the elevator, and Ray pressed the 11th-floor button. He planned to begin the tour with the fixed income group, just as Marty wanted. There was a big screen with market indices so they could watch the whole broad market. Overall, it reminded Marty of the bond trading floor at Fidelity. Raymond James was one of the best, and it looked like they were doing a ton of business.

Next stop was mutual funds. About twenty-five reps covered all mutual funds. Any statistic that you wanted was at your fingertips. Reps could even run analytical and forecasts based on the funds' actual performance. They even traded electronically traded funds (ETFs). They kept extremely good records, so there was no problem finding the cost basis. That was a huge problem at Primevest. If someone sold a security, they had to know how much they had invested in it so they could determine how much tax they owed on any capital gain.

Several floors down, the next stop was the insurance department. It was lunchtime, and they were taking Marty and Heidi out. Ray said he wanted them to spend time with the insurance team, so he invited two people from the department to come along.

Marty was not sure why he had invited them. She wondered, "Heidi and I both had a book of clients with variable annuities, but nothing more. Does he have a new product on the horizon? Otherwise, why invite them?" She was intrigued and felt if there was a better product, she wanted to learn about it.

Ray had planned a seafood lunch. Since they were in Tampa, they might as well enjoy one of the best restaurants. It was very posh, and waiters were running around everywhere. Before the appetizers arrived, one of the insurance gurus spoke up, "Do either of you know anything about variable life insurance?"

At the same time, they both said, "No."

"We have a virtual training department, which allows anyone to log on using their computer and create scenarios for clients based on how much money they want to invest. The program automatically spits out a death benefit. Withdrawing from a variable life contract is tax-free. The beneficiaries will receive tax-free distributions upon the person's death. Inside the policies are mutual funds just like your variable annuities."

Both women said they would like to experience the virtual department when they returned to Raymond James' campus. The new product sounded too good to be true, and the commissions were off the charts.

On the way back, Marty's cell phone rang. It was Lily Francis. She said Tim had been in an accident and was at Mesquite Community Hospital. She had little information, except that she needed to get home as soon as possible.

Ray and Heidi sensed something was wrong, then Marty said, "Ray, we need to go straight to the airport. My husband has been in a terrible accident and is in the hospital."

"I'm so sorry. I'll have a driver take you immediately, and we will get someone to go to your hotel, pack everything, and overnight your bags."

Marty felt as if she were about to explode. She was so afraid for her husband. What if he was in a coma? What if he had lost a limb? She couldn't keep the bad thoughts out of her head, became extremely anxious, and grabbed Heidi's hand.

Heidi tried to comfort her by saying it's all in God's hands now. "Let's pray together," and the two of them bowed their heads and prayed. Marty was scared to death, but she prayed with all of her might.

The flight home was excruciating. Marty was consumed with worry about Tim. They landed, and when Marty got home, she jumped into her car and drove as fast as she could to the hospital. She went to the front desk and said that she was Mrs. Rooney, and her husband was in the ICU. The nurse quickly escorted her through the double doors to the ICU waiting room. All Marty could think about was if he was going to make it. How would her life be without him? She saw that he had a bandage on his arm, but the rest of his body was covered.

One of the doctors came in and said, "Your doctor, Dr. Caddel, came as fast as he could when he got the call and has been with him all night. He never left Tim's side."

Marty wanted to know how much of his body had been hurt and what had happened.

He took Marty's hand, "Tim has been in a motorcycle accident, which wasn't his fault. Somebody pulled out in front of him, and he slid under the car. We were able to stabilize his breathing, and he is under a ventilator blanket. Although his condition is serious, we feel good about the prognosis. That's all we know at this point. Please try not to worry, we have him under close observation."

She had to sit down because her legs were so weak. She thought, "How could he be out riding on that Harley Davidson when he knew she didn't want him on that bike? That was it. That Hog is history." This determination gave her strength because it made her mad.

After regaining some strength, she thought it was best to go down to the cafeteria, get a cup of coffee, and wait.

Dr. Caddel was waiting for her when she came back from the cafeteria. She rushed towards him. "Marty, Tim has suffered a massive concussion, and he might be out for a while. He is not in a coma, which is typical with this kind of concussion. He has a broken right arm and a bad burn on his right leg where he went under the car. When the emergency team got to him, he was still stuck underneath, so the wound was severe. We don't know the full extent of the damage to his leg. We have no way of knowing when he might wake up, so I encourage you to go home and get some rest, and if anything changes, I will call you."

She asked him, "Can you move Tim to a private room with a couch or fold-out bed so I can be by his side when he wakes up?" Marty wanted to be sure she was there.

"No, for now we need to keep him quarantined in the ICU."

Marty took Dr. Caddell's advice and headed for the parking lot. She felt like a zombie, with no idea what time it was. She wasn't sure she had the strength to drive. She started up her Lexus and headed home.

Ryan ran out to greet her. He was such a happy boy. She decided not to tell him what was going on but only that Daddy would be gone for a few days on business. Lily Francis had not said a word about the accident. That's the way Marty wanted it. That's the way Tim would've wanted it, as well. Why cause worry to their child? Marty could do enough worrying for the two of them.

Ryan was excited to show her what he had done at school. He was quite the little artist and had drawn her a sunset. Marty's heart ached at the thought that Tim might not see another sunset. She told herself she wouldn't think that way and that she would wake up the next day, and he would be awake too.

She told Lily Francis she was going to take a sleeping pill and sleep in Ryan's room beside him. She surely needed a good night's sleep, but she wanted to make sure everybody was safe.

The next day, Marty had to check in at work, so she called Robert Halsey and told him about the accident. He said, "Take as much time as you need. We will be here when you get back." Robert was a man of faith and said he would be praying for Tim.

Marty decided to eat a light breakfast before leaving for the hospital. There had been no phone calls, so apparently nothing had changed. She dreaded going to the hospital and seeing Tim in the ICU. She felt helpless. There was nothing she could do or say to wake him. She wondered if he was dreaming. She wondered if he could remember the accident. She just wanted him to wake up and be okay.

Upon her arrival, the doctor came out to greet her, "There has been no change, but the good thing is he is breathing on his own, and we were able to take him off the ventilator. There doesn't appear to be anything wrong with his lungs. We were afraid maybe he had broken a rib and punctured his lung, but that fear has passed."

Marty questioned, "Why is he still in the ICU if no ventilator is needed? Why can't he go to a private room?"

"We are still monitoring him because of the bad surface burns."

She knew that Tim would not be in the ICU forever. She wondered how many days he could go without eating. She determined that he would eventually leave this hospital and be a strong man again. She remained confident and kept praying.

She picked up the Bible she had brought from home and sat down by his side. She placed her hand over his and began reading scripture to him even though he was unconscious. She had been reading for quite a while when she felt some sort of movement in his hand. She ran to the nurses' station and yelled, "Tim is moving."

One of the doctors came running to check on Tim, but he looked no different. He pulled his chart and said, "It was probably just a reflex." Then he added, "There was an indication that his eyes were moving in his sleep. That's a good indication. I feel it is only a matter of time before he wakes up."

The doctor seemed sure and continued, "Tim's situation is not life-threatening. However, he will most likely need skin grafts on the burned areas. Other than that, I'm confident he will be back to normal very soon.

Marty watched Tim's eyes as she read the Bible, looking for any sign of response or a passage he might respond to. She started with the 23rd Psalm, and as she read, she glanced over to see if his eyes were moving. When she finished, she saw a slight twitch, and it appeared his eyes were moving. She didn't know how God was getting through to him, but He was. Next, she read the Lord's Prayer, and there was more movement in his eyes.

She hit the button, and a nurse responded. Excitedly, she said, "Tim's eyes are moving, please ask the doctor to come in."

When the doctor arrived, he said, "Tim's eye movement is a good sign. It is not unusual for people in a coma to hear what is being said. I'm not certain, but it seems he heard what you were saying. I think a good dose of glucose might wake him up."

The doctor instructed the nurse, and they started feeding him glucose through his drip bag.

After about ten minutes, Marty could feel Tim's hand moving, so she leaned over and kissed him, and to her amazement, his eyes popped open, and he said, "Where am I? How did I get here?"

Marty started crying, and the nurse ran to get the doctor. Tim had been asleep for three days, which wasn't that bad considering his injuries. He had slept right through most of the pain. Now that he was awake, he couldn't remember anything that had happened. The doctor was shocked and told her that this was a great sign.

Finally, they moved Tim out of the ICU and into a private room. Marty was there waiting with his comfortable pajamas, house shoes, and personal items. She wanted him to feel at home because she knew he would heal faster. She really wanted to take him home and hire a private nurse to watch him, but he still had to be looked after for the burns that he had suffered.

Marty got a call from Robert Halsey checking on Tim. He understood it was a motorcycle accident, and it wasn't Tim's fault. He recommended Harry Walton as a good attorney. He said Tim had a lawsuit and could win a lot of money for what he had suffered. He said Harry was a friend of his and a top attorney in Dallas. He said he knew he could win the case if anyone could.

So, Marty thanked him, wrote down Harry's phone number, and promised to call him. She told Robert that Tim had been moved out of the ICU and was now in a private room. Robert asked what hospital it was, so Marty told him. Robert immediately had his secretary order a plant and had it delivered. He thought that's the least he could do, but he was still praying for Tim and Marty.

While Tim was sleeping, Marty called Harry Walton. She got his secretary and said Robert Halsey had referred her to him. The secretary put her on hold for a minute or two before Mr. Walton picked up. He asked what he could do for her, and she told him about the accident.

He was silent until she completed her story, then said, "I'm confident that I can be of assistance; substantial payments are sometimes awarded to the victim to offset future disabilities. We will need to involve the doctors. Would you like to set a time for me to come over and meet with you?" Somewhat stunned by his positive response, she said, "Most definitely!"

They set a time and decided it would be best to meet outside of the hospital at a local restaurant.

While Tim was eating, Marty spoke to him, "I talked to an attorney today. Robert Halsey referred me to Harry Walton, who is evidently a hotshot accident attorney. He told me that he could help us and agreed to meet. After talking to him, I feel we might have a case."

She leaned over and kissed him, "I'll be back in a little while. We are going to meet for lunch, and I plan to return with good news. Who knows, maybe one day we will be millionaires."

Mr. Walton was a heavyset man who wore impeccable suits. He looked like he was made of money. He had won famous lawsuits collecting millions of dollars for his clients and, coincidentally, for himself. You could see his ads running on TV, and some people called him an ambulance chaser. Marty couldn't care less—the only thing she planned to call him was a "Godsend." The medical bills were piling up, and they had no idea about rehabilitation and what that would entail.

Howard and Marty got a table and ordered lunch. Howard pulled out a brochure about his company. "I usually don't make house calls unless it's for a friend, which I consider Robert to be. Here is some generic information on our company. We have twenty-six attorneys, so I rarely work cases. Do you know the insurance company for the lady who hit Tim?"

He wanted to know whether Marty had contacted them yet and whether she had received a response. Marty said, "Yes, I contacted them, but they acted nonchalantly, saying a case like this is pretty basic and they would be willing to talk to her about an out-of-court settlement."

Little did they know she planned to hire a lion as an attorney.

Mr. Walton said with authority, "Don't worry, I will take it from there. Please don't contact them again, and don't take any calls from them. I should be able to provide you with some options very soon."

Harry started doing his research, and upon reading the police report, he discovered the driver who had hit Tim was under the influence of alcohol. He knew from experience that this meant they could get more money. At a minimum, he planned to have the company pay all of Tim's previous and future hospital bills. With a little cynical smile, he murmured, "I'm going after them for the max."

Tim was recovering nicely and slowly reclaiming his position as king of his castle. Marty smiled and said, "Alright, you can act like Hugh Hefner for a time, but not forever."

Marty could tell he was really getting back to his old self when he asked for fast food. He was craving Arby's roast beef sandwiches with their creamy and zesty horsey sauce. Not wanting to deny his every wish, Marty located the nearest Arby's and loaded up. He had been on such a strict diet that he had lost about fifteen pounds, and she wanted to put that weight back on him as quickly as possible.

As she was preparing to leave, he yelled, "Think you could stop by Wendy's on the way back and get me a Frosty?"

"OK." Marty thought it might be time to see if he could drive.

Ray Willis was calling to check on Tim. He was also checking in with Marty to see if she had made any decision about moving to Raymond James. He knew she had a lot on her mind, but he wanted her to remember what was waiting for her. She could have her own firm, make her own hours, and keep 90% of the income. He had questions about Heidi, as well.

"How is Heidi doing? Do you think she will be joining you when you open your new office?"

Marty had always wanted to own her own firm. Now, the deal with Raymond James appeared to be the chance of a lifetime, but she knew the timing had to be right.

"No," she thought, "It needs to be perfect."

Marty called Heidi, "Ray called and asked if we had decided. I told him we haven't had any time to discuss it because of the situation with Tim. Heidi, Tim is making real progress. I think I'm going to sign the contract and put the plan into motion. Are you with me?"

Heidi responded with excitement, "I'm ready to move when you are. I'm happy at the bank, but I'm really looking forward to earning higher commissions."

Marty felt this would be the perfect time to handover her book of clients from the bank to Brad. They had been unable to transfer his business from Edward Jones, so he basically had to start from scratch. She knew he could handle her accounts; it would be a nice trade-off for him, and it would fill the hole at the bank if Marty exited stage left. She had to decide whether to stay at the bank, given the constraints, or to open her own firm. Could she make it on her own?

Harry Walton called to update them on the lawsuit. He said the hospital had released the records, and it looked like Tim was going to be on a cane for the rest of his life. The accident had shaved off part of his foot so that he would walk with a limp for the rest of his life.

It had been several months since the accident, and Marty thought Tim was walking funny. Now, she knew why. Dr. Caddell had not said anything about him needing a cane, but now she understood what the rest of his life looked like. Tim couldn't run, which was a real setback. He loved to get out and run a couple of miles every day. She wondered what the lawsuit was worth in dollars.

Harry went on to say, "It is a big deal when we are dealing with a lifelong injury, and considering that the driver was intoxicated changes the game. It strengthens our case and merits us asking for the maximum payout. You will likely be looking at around two million, and my fee is about one-third of the payment. It is best to settle without going to court, which would save you and Tim a lot of time and grief. But I can't guarantee anything."

Marty thought that was high, but when you consider how the accident had changed Tim, she felt it was worth it. If he could get that amount, they could basically retire. However, she also thought it might be nice to build her own complex. She could own a building and her own practice.

"So, our payout will be approximately $1.4 million?" She asked.

"No, the $2 million is net of my fee."

They never expected that much. They would've been happy with one million or less. There was a silver lining to this dark cloud. Unfortunately, Tim would walk with a limp, but at least he would walk. They both agreed they would accept Mr. Walton's suggestion.

"Marty," Tim said, holding her hand. "I couldn't care less about the limp, the only thing that matters is that I can still hold you and make love to you without any problem. That was the main thing I worried about in the hospital. I dreamed of our naked bodies lying next to each other. We need a break, so why don't we plan one of our special getaway weekends?"

Tim was hoping for another baby, but he wasn't sure Marty was ready — she was in business mode. Marty melted into his arms, thinking, "Oh, you have no idea the fun we are going to have playing around again."

Tim was feeling a little guilty that the settlement could be so much when all he had was a limp, but he knew that was lawfare. He could buy Marty that building she wanted and fulfill her heart's desire.

She called her attorney to set up a meeting to discuss the contract from Raymond James. She needed to understand her liabilities. She had already prepared a spreadsheet of her potential expenses and overhead.

"I'm ready to sign and find a building."

After reviewing her contract, her attorney, Jackson Wallace, covered the particulars, specifically, the liabilities she might incur. He explained, "You have errors-and-omissions insurance built into the contract that protects you for any trading errors totaling $30,000 or less. The bonus they are offering looks good, but if you leave the firm for any reason within the first year, you will need to refund the amount."

She thought it was reasonable and wasn't worried about refunding the bonus; she knew whatever firm she chose would be a lifetime partnership. She had no plans ever to move her business to another broker-dealer. This was the time, and she was going to make it happen.

Jackson told her it was time to sign the contract, "You have done an extremely good job on the due diligence, and I feel confident in what you are planning. I believe you will be highly successful. In fact, once you are up and running, I would like to talk about my own portfolio and, while we're at it, discuss the firm's 401(k)."

Marty signed the contract and handed it back to Jackson. "Please send it to Raymond James." Then smiled, "The ink isn't even dry, and I already have my first customer."

The next step was talking to Robert Halsey. She wanted to leave the bank in good standing. She had built a large department that was bringing in over $100,000 a month in fees. The bank had thirteen licensed registered reps and three licensed sales assistants, 13,000 accounts, and over $250 million in assets under management through Primevest. The quarterly recurring income was $25,000.

Ray Willis confirmed he had received the contract, and it was in good order. He let her know that whenever she was ready, they would transfer her license, and she could open her branch. The framework was laid for Marty to open her own office of securities jurisdiction. Now, the next step was finding a location. She planned to leave the bank one day and open her own branch the next.

Marty contacted a local commercial real estate agent, Karen Williamson, whom she met at a Chamber of Commerce meeting in Rockwall. She was very impressive and worked for Ebby Halliday, a company with an excellent reputation.

Marty called her office and set up an appointment. Marty knew exactly what kind of building she wanted. Karen had access to the entire metroplex, so she felt she would be the best candidate for this project.

They sat down, and Marty explained her intentions, "I would like to find a building in the suburbs and far enough away from the bank that we don't cross paths. I envision something like an old red brick schoolhouse with plenty of open space. I plan for everyone to work out of an office, not a cubicle."

She planned to divide the building into different departments. She would give independent brokers a chance to work out of a large facility with state-of-the-art technology.

When Marty got home that night, Tim was waiting at the door. "I have some good news and some better news. Harry Walton called, "We won the lawsuit! The settlement is going to be $2.25 million."

Marty was shocked. They had just become automatic millionaires over something so tragic. God had come through again. They were set for life, and the timing couldn't have been better. Marty had the money to buy her own building.

Marty knew what she wanted the building to look like. She wanted a lot of offices with different departments and a real receptionist, one who answered the phone, not some pre-programmed answering machine. She always felt that having a live person answering the phone provided a personal touch people liked.

A week had passed since she and Karen Williamson had met, so she called to see if she had made any progress.

"I have a few options for you to consider. I have not been able to locate a red-brick schoolhouse, but I did find an old red-brick warehouse you might want to look at. The property is in Mesquite, about ten minutes from where you live in Sunnyvale. I have another, more modern building that might suit your needs. If you like, we can meet tomorrow at one, tour the warehouse, and then I can set up the other for a three o'clock tour."

The old red brick warehouse was exactly what Marty was looking for. She had a vision of what the building would look like, and this turned out exactly as she had imagined. Another God thing.

The building was large enough to house the various departments and employees Marty wanted to hire. There was going to be a ping pong and pool table in the lobby, and she could easily place a receptionist at the front entrance. There was plenty of room to build a bar behind the reception desk so she could serve any kind of drink they wanted. Marty was going to call the receptionist a concierge, an ambassador for the firm. She would not only meet and greet, but also serve. She would be a ten in looks, a Dallas Cowboy cheerleader type.

Marty envisioned this as a first-class, full-service brokerage. She wanted to build a full kitchen and serving area so employees could eat good meals every day and invite clients to dine in. There would be plenty of seating and a large table that could seat twenty for client events. Employees and tenants would only have to pay a meager amount and wouldn't have to leave the building. This would be much more appealing than driving somewhere only to pay higher restaurant prices every day. Plus, a good home-cooked meal was worth paying for. She knew that with Tim's restaurant experience, he could hire the cooks, a kitchen manager, and help manage it for her.

Marty looked over at Karen and said, "I envision this to be a great spot for a first-class, full-service brokerage. How much are they asking?"

Karen said, "As is, $195,000."

She and Tim had budgeted $100,000 for the renovation, hoping to be all in for less than $300,000. Marty asked Karen to counter at $189,000, but the owners refused to budge, so Marty agreed to accept their price. The deal was finalized after the attorneys haggled over the paperwork.

The building was theirs, and the dream of turning it into a mega-warehouse of financial offerings was becoming a reality.

They needed to hire a contractor, and one of their neighbors in Sunnyvale recommended a company he had used to renovate a commercial building, which had done an excellent job. The company was named Emery Construction, so Marty and Tim made an appointment. The first step in completing the building.

Marty wanted to see if their designer could envision her dream. Could they build a modern but comfortable office building that didn't feel like an office building? She asked Karen Williamson to get involved because she knew the building and could coordinate a rendition with Emery Construction in anticipation of their appointment. They wanted to see what their plan would be. Marty and Tim knew they would only be looking at sketches, but they would share their ideas, and that is what Marty wanted to see. Was Emery Construction on the same page?

Tim thought it was a good idea for Marty to sit down and map out each floor of the building. He knew there was to be an elevator to the second floor. He wondered which floor Marty would take for her own. Also, who did she want to occupy the space, and how many brokers did she want to hire? She had mentioned four brokers and two licensed sales assistants, but otherwise, he did not know her plans. He agreed to oversee the cafeteria, set up the kitchen, and design the table layout.

Marty had definite plans. She would hire four brokers, starting with Heidi Becker. Her office and three brokers would be on the second floor or mezzanine level. The offices would be all glass with curtains that could be drawn for privacy. On the first floor, she decided to hire two concierges, and they would be the first point of contact for anyone entering the building. They would back up the sales assistants.

She wanted to invite a property and casualty insurance company to rent space from her. Everyone needed car insurance. She also wanted to rent an office to a CPA. Everybody had taxes due. She would rent space to companies that provided services but were not in competition with her or anybody else in her building. Her vision was to create a one-stop shop. All companies would be connected to the central phone bank, and after hours, the phones would be answered by an answering service. The only voicemail would be for the individuals.

The decor would be mid-century. Marty was born in 1955 and loved the era. This would be a fun place to work and to visit. Unlike a stuffy office building in downtown Dallas, where everything was glass and chrome, this building would be welcoming, with ample parking just outside the door. She wanted a children's area on the first floor with cubbyholes so kids could grab toys and play while their parents were at work with their advisers. She wasn't entirely sure how that idea would work, but she wanted to include children. Her son, Ryan, who would soon be a teenager, suggested that some old video games, such as Pac-Man and Tetris, be put in the children's area.

The building was 10,000 square feet, with 5,000 square feet per floor. The main attraction would be the boardroom and its table. It was Marty's lifelong dream to be president and sit at the head of a boardroom table; to do so would signal that she had reached the pinnacle of her career. She was still unsure how it would all work, but she somehow knew that God would make it work. There were no accidents. Even Einstein was quoted as saying, "God didn't put dice in the universe."

Marty and Tim needed to make this happen as quickly as possible. They met with Emery Construction and showed them her hand-drawn layout sketch. Charlie Hawkins, who headed up the group, said, "This looks like a fine plan. Everything appears to be logically laid out and logistically sound. What is the purpose of such a large kitchen in the back on the main floor?"

Marty explained, "We want a cafeteria to service the whole building. The kitchen staff will prepare lunch daily, and we will use the space for private functions in the evening. Charlie, it needs to be nice. No, it must be fabulous."

She included her ideas about creating a mid-century modern look. Charlie thought that was an excellent idea and believed it would set the building apart.

Next, Charlie asked, "What is your vision for the exterior?"

Marty wanted it to be welcoming, easily accessible, and beautiful. She envisioned park benches outside and picnic tables next to the building, with umbrella tables, so they could eat outside or get a breath of fresh air. The old warehouse had parking spaces all the way around the building. She thought it would be best for the executives to park in the back of the building, leaving the front spaces for customers. She wanted the building to feel like an old house, so plenty of landscaping would be necessary. Green ivy was already growing up on one side of the building, and she wanted to keep it.

Proudly she declared, "I'm naming the building, The Ivy House."

The team at Emery was impressed with Marty's rendition of the building. They had never encountered anybody who knew exactly what they wanted and could express it so well. Everyone in the meeting knew exactly what Marty wanted and said they would create blueprints for her approval before beginning construction.

Curious, Marty asked, "What will be the project cost?"

Charlie spoke up and said, "That will be presented along with the blueprint. Once we have the plans drawn, we will be able to determine the cost of the materials and the finish-out. However, based on what we have discussed thus far and my previous experience, I would estimate the cost to be somewhere in the $80,000 range."

"Charlie, this will be an all-cash deal; we will not be borrowing any money for the project. If you can keep the estimate below $80,000 and to my specifications, I feel sure we can make a deal."

She really liked Charlie. He was a crusty old construction guy and shot straight from the hip. No bullshit with him. She liked the ruggedness about him. He was the type who would probably be active on the job instead of standing off to the side, watching all the worker bees. He probably wore overalls with a pencil in his pocket and a folding yardstick in his back pocket.

The meeting with Emery Construction was productive, and the team let them know it would take about six months to renovate the building once Marty approved the drawings.

Marty and Tim were pleased to hear the lower estimate. They were rolling in cash after the lawsuit, so they had no worries about the cost of the building or filling it with the right people. Tim had full confidence that Marty would fulfill her dream, and intended to do whatever was necessary on his part to make it happen.

He absolutely adored her. In fact, the first time he told her so was on their third date. She made him stop the car, and he said, "Are you going to vomit?"

Marty laughed, "No, I just wanted us to stop so I could hear you say that again. Tim, I adore you."

She decided it was time to call Brad and tell him the truth. Afterall, he was going to play a big part in her move. Marty was trying to get her ducks in a row about her decision to move to Raymond James.

When Brad picked up the phone, Marty was ready, "Brad, I want to share some exciting news. Tim and I have decided the time is right for me to be independent. We put an offer in on a building, and I'm going to go out on my own. With your approval, I am planning to turn over all my clients to you and suggest to Robert Halsey that you take my place. It would require you to sit for the Series 24 test and obtain your license. What do you think?"

Brad was taken aback. Starting over had been challenging; he was open to anything that would make his life easier.

"Well, I don't know what to say, but hell yes."

She contacted Robert Halsey to request a meeting, and they agreed on a time.

"Robert, I don't know how else to say this, but I'm venturing out on my own. I want you to know how much I have enjoyed working with you and everyone at the bank."

Robert hesitated before saying, "Marty, this comes as a complete shock. What are we going to do? Who could we get to take your place?"

"Well, I would never leave without having a smooth transition plan in place and making sure I left on good terms. When we couldn't get Brad's business transferred from Edward Jones, he had to start all over and has been working diligently. I would be willing to hand over all my clients to him. Why don't we have him test for and secure his Series 24 license, and then ask whether he would like to take over as branch supervisor in my place? This would change his life and put the bank in good hands."

Marty found it hard to tell Robert about her plans. She held her breath waiting to hear his response. If he agreed, he would surely do the right thing and give Brad the same title.

Robert rose from his seat and looked out of the window in his office, but remained silent.

After what seemed like an eternity, Robert turned and said, "Marty, you never cease to amaze me. I think that would be an excellent idea. In fact, why don't we offer Brad the same title?"

Marty let out a sigh of relief. The final piece had just fallen into place.

She put the plan into action, everything worked as planned, and soon was operating like clockwork. Brad got his license and began serving Marty's clients, which made him happy and took the pressure off.

Marty got a call from her old friend, Linda Newkirk, at Eaton Vance mutual funds. Linda was hosting a big party in the ballroom at her swanky downtown condo and wanted to invite Marty.

"Hey Marty, I'm planning an Asian fusion theme. Won't you join me? There will be my usual supply of stockbrokers and financial planners to shmooze with."

Linda always put on a good party, and the financial world loved to attend. It would be an excellent place for Marty to recruit discreetly. What a perfect opportunity to round out her crew. She needed three more brokers to be independent advisers under her 0SJ.

At the party, she started collecting business cards. She moved through the room like melting ice cream, covering every nook and cranny, looking for the best of the best. She knew Linda had statistics on all those in attendance, but she thought she'd better meet them in person, decide who she liked, and then ask Linda what she thought.

Her pockets were bulging with cards. She met with over fifty advisers, but only ten showed promise. Several were from banks that would be a good fit, especially after they learned they could earn a 40% commission without having to work out of a bank lobby. As the evening drew to a close, she thanked Linda for a fabulous time and headed to the street where she had the valet bring her Lexus.

The prospects were promising, and her plan was coming together. It was time to do some serious recruiting. Marty had already jumped through some significant hurdles. Finding the building was a big one; now filling it was another. She had written out her plan on how best to approach the building.

She wanted to secure rental income by luring an insurance agent and a certified public accountant to lease space in the building. These were the first and most essential steps to her plan. She figured she could charge them $3,000 a month and ask for a five-year contract.

She had always used Farmers Insurance, and she adored her rep, Greg Harding. He had an office in Hurst, which was forty-five minutes away, but thought he might consider moving. If not, he might consider leasing space and hiring an agent to work through him.

The obvious choice for a CPA was Alfredo Lopez, who had handled their taxes for over ten years. He was in Mesquite, so the office would be a perfect location for him. He only had a secretary and a boring office, so she was certain she could work out a deal with him.

Wasting no time, she picked up the phone and called Greg Harding with Farmers Insurance. Greg's secretary answered the phone and said Greg was with somebody. She asked if there was anything she could help with.

"No thanks, I need to talk to Greg directly. Please ask him to return my call."

Greg would be tough to negotiate with because he had been at that location for more than 20 years. Originally, Marty opened an account with him because she lived in that part of town. Rarely was there a reason to see your insurance agent in person. Now that she lived in another part of town, they did business over the phone. All transactions were digital anyway, which might be her saving grace when trying to entice him to move. Afterall he would be just a phone call away from any of his clients.

Greg called back, and Marty got right to the point, "I just completed building a massive financial complex, and would like you to consider leasing an office. There will be financial advisors and a CPA firm. My vision was to create a one-stop financial powerhouse that meets all our clients' needs. I will have two concierges to greet your clients, and you will have access to the dining room and boardroom. You will have your own private parking space and final say on the office setup."

Greg congratulated Marty on her accomplishment and said, "A financial one-stop shop is very appealing. Look, I have been in Hurst for over twenty years, and moving my practice doesn't make sense. However, the Mesquite Branch of Farmers Insurance might be a perfect fit. What is the rent?"

Marty told him $3,000 per month. He responded, "Interesting, my overhead is well over $6,000. a month. That's a pretty good deal. Why don't you hold off on contacting the Mesquite branch? I might have an idea for expanding my practice. Mesquite's population could support two agents. Give me a little time to think things through. I will need to check with my corporate office to make sure I don't violate any radius clause."

There was a lot to consider, and Greg was very interested, but he didn't know how he would approach it. He knew that he could not go personally, so he called his corporate office, "Is it okay to have an agent working under my branch work at another location? Does it matter if there is another Farmers Insurance branch within ten miles?"

The person he was talking to said he had no idea and that he would have to transfer Greg to the right person. He felt Larry Hillis, the recruiter for Farmers, might be the right person to talk to.

Greg said, "I will call Mr. Hillis tomorrow. Thanks for the contact."

Greg thought the smartest thing he could do was call Ken Miller, the Farmers agent in Mesquite, and tell him about Marty's building and what she wanted to do. Ethically, it was the right thing to do. Greg really didn't need another agent, and $3000 per month was a lot of overhead for an agent just starting his business.

Greg called Ken and reached his secretary. The Farmers agents all knew one another and attended the same conventions and continuing education classes. They were a tight-knit group, like a big family, and they did not compete with one another. They felt like there was plenty of territory for everybody. Greg knew Ken well and thought he had good business in Mesquite and would be perfect for Marty's building.

"Hey Ken, Greg Harding, I've got some exciting news for you. I think you know Marty Bledsoe. Well, she has opened a place in Mesquite called The Ivy House and filled it with a powerhouse of financial professionals, stockbrokers, and certified financial planners. She wants to include an insurance agent in her building. She contacted me to see if I might be interested. Of course, I can't take her up on the offer, since it's in your territory, I thought I would run it by you to see if you might be interested. She is asking $3,000 a month, which includes concierge service, a boardroom, a full gourmet kitchen, a dining room, and private parking. There's ample space for you and your secretary, and you can design the space however you see fit. The building is just now being renovated."

"Greg, that sounds like an unbelievable deal at $3000 per month. I want to drive over and take a look. What's the address? "

Greg gave Marty a quick call, "Hey Marty, I need the address to The Ivy House. I'm unable to take advantage of your offer, but I may know someone who can. Ken Miller is the Farmers agent in Mesquite, so I called and told him about your offer. He wants to come over and see the building."

"I'd be happy to meet him and walk him through."

"Let me check with Ken, but it might be good for you to give him a call. I think it would be better for the two of you to talk."

Marty contacted Ken and scheduled a meeting at the El Chico Restaurant in Mesquite. She had learned that everything looked better after a full stomach.

"After lunch, I'll take you over to The Ivy House for a tour. Be prepared to wear a hard hat--the contractors will be actively working."

Ken said curiously, "What other businesses will be in the building, and why do you think Farmers Insurance is the best agency to have there?

Marty suggested, "Why don't we discuss everything over lunch, and I'll bring a blueprint of the building for you to look at."

She intentionally suggested they meet at 1:00 to avoid the lunch crowd and to discuss business in a quieter environment. She was so excited that he was open to the idea. She felt that if she were successful in landing a CPA and an insurance company, her plan would succeed. It seemed like a natural fit for them to join forces with stockbrokers. If she pulled it off, it would be a real feat.

Marty gathered all her statistics on the building and on how she envisioned the companies working together. It would be like one big family, with no competition. She planned to set up an incentive referral program. All her clients needed car insurance, housing insurance, tax preparation, and financial advice. She envisioned the companies hosting events together. What a wonderful way to join businesses with client sharing. It had never been done before. Marty would be the first.

It was one o'clock, and Marty was right on time, but Ken was running late. She took a table and browsed the menu. She looked for something she didn't have to use her fingers for, so tacos were out. However, she couldn't resist chowing down on the chips and hot sauce. That was the best part of the whole meal at El Chico. Ken showed up, took a seat, and apologized for being late, saying he couldn't find parking. He appeared eager to talk to Marty.

"Are they giving away money in this place?" he asked, and they both laughed. It was a very popular Mexican restaurant, but the crowd eventually subsided. Ken glanced at the luncheon specials, and Marty said she had already decided on what she would get. The waitress came, took their order, and made sure they had plenty of iced tea.

Marty brought her attaché instead of a purse. She reached over and pulled out the blueprint, which had been reduced in size so she could carry it around and show it off. She moved the napkins and silverware over and laid the blueprint in front of Ken. She pointed to the area where his office would be located on the first floor. She told him there would be a marquee out front with a scrolling sign, so he would have signage along with everyone else on the street level.

"You can do whatever you want with the space regarding signage, but I'd prefer you run it by me first. I want to ensure everything is consistent and professional. I think the signage will bring in a lot of customers. No one has a scrolling sign, and we will be able to run stock quotes across it."

"Your plan to create a mega financial institution sounds like a fabulous opportunity. I would love to be part of a one-stop shop. Greg told me what you were asking for in rent, and it's about half of what I am currently paying. My secretary works separately from me, so would there be room for her as well?

"Of course."

Marty picked up the tab with her platinum American Express card, which she was proud of. She could buy a Porsche with that card if she wanted to.

Ken noticed the card and knew it was a status symbol; platinum meant unlimited credit. Ken was beginning to respect Marty in a way he had never respected a woman. She appeared to be a natural-born leader, professional, and someone who could get the job done. He felt she was a go-getter who left no details unnoticed.

He liked her and had already made up his mind that he was going to take the office, but he didn't want to get ahead of himself; they hadn't toured the complex, and it all sounded almost too good to be true. He decided not to say anything to Marty.

They jumped into Marty's Lexus and drove to the building. The construction workers were everywhere, so they parked where they could avoid the ruckus. The crew was installing the grand front double doors, framed in mahogany. Marty thought the doors were a good look for the front of the building, and they matched the brick, making the place look a little like a southern mansion.

Ken was speechless. He had no idea that the building was so large.

"The building is 10,000 square feet, and I'm sorry that the small blueprint I showed you of the interior didn't express what the exterior looked like; you really needed to see it up close.

Ken thought the place looked like it was made of money. Lots of money. He was definitely going to sign on.

"I have three months left on my current rental contract; how long do you expect the construction to take?

"That should coincide nicely with the completion of The Ivy House."

"I'm in, sign me up."

She had her first tenant ready to sign a contract, so she needed to move on to her second target, her CPA, Alfredo Lopez. He had always done a good job and was fair with his fees. His current office was in a dingy strip center, where Marty dreaded using the restroom. It was obviously a men's restroom because there was never any soap in the dispenser. She had to dry her hands on toilet paper. It was disgusting. If he moved to her building, he would think he was in Shangri-La.

She decided to call him and invite him to her home office. She and Tim lived in a stunning mansion, and she thought he might be impressed. Tim had built it especially for her with all the computers and phones that she needed. They would meet on her turf, where she felt like she had more power than anywhere else. Not that she needed it, but she considered it a mortal cinch.

She called him, and his secretary answered and put her through to Alfredo.

"Alfredo, I need to meet with you as soon as possible. Do you mind stopping by my home office?"

"Hey Marty, always good hearing from you. Of course, is something wrong that I should be aware of?"

"No, not at all. How does Friday at one work for you?"

Alfredo responded, "That works for me."

He was curious about why Marty wanted to see him at her home. He thought the worst, that maybe she was going to fire him.

She planned for them to meet after lunch, so the kitchen would be all cleaned up and the house would be spotless. She wanted to impress him and, at the same time, wanted him to feel important and needed as she introduced her new adventure.

She thought Friday would never get there. She was so eager and excited to talk to Alfredo about the opportunity of moving to her building. He was not only on time, but arrived 15 minutes early. She liked his punctuality; Marty's rule was to always arrive 15 minutes early for appointments.

Lily Frances answered the door while Marty waited in her office. She guided him past the swimming pool and their gourmet kitchen. Alfredo was taking it all in. He had never been in a house that big. He silently wondered, "How many bedrooms does she have. She must have family living with her." Having done their taxes for so many years, he knew that they were wealthy, but he didn't realize how wealthy.

Lily Francis tapped Marty's open office door. Marty motioned for him to come in and directed him to sit. She was deliberately acting as if she were on a phone call. As she hung up, she stretched out her hand. Her office was very impressive, displaying the many awards she had earned over the years. Pictures graced the office walls, which would soon be moved to her building.

"Alfredo, would you like anything to drink? Lily Francis will be happy to get you anything you want."

A little shaken, he managed to say, "Bottled water would be nice."

"How about sparkling water?" Before he could respond she told Lily Francis to bring two glasses of sparkling water. Now, she was ready to get down to business. Marty had him right where she wanted him.

"Alfredo, I'm afraid our taxes are going to be more complex; I'm expanding my business. I'm going independent and opening my own Office of Securities Jurisdiction. That means I can hire brokers to work under me and capture some of their commissions. The legal term is revenue sharing. I have been planning this move for quite some time, and have purchased a rather large building in Mesquite. I'm building a financial powerhouse, and I would like you to be part of my plan. I want you to relocate and rent an office from me."

He laughed and said, "I thought you were going to fire me."

"Quite the contrary, for the past ten years, you have done an excellent job on our taxes. I'm creating a one-stop shop for my clients and need a solid CPA. I have already signed a lease with a Farmers Insurance agent. The rent will be $3,000 a month, and your office will be big enough for you and your secretary. You can build out the space any way you want."

Alfredo's mind was spinning. Since he was already in Mesquite, his clients probably wouldn't mind him moving to a new office, especially if it offered a better location than his current one.

Breaking his train of thought, Marty asked, "How much are you paying in rent?"

"I'm currently at $2,500."

Marty knew the time had come for her to quit talking and let him respond. She leaned back in her chair and went silent.

"I'm a little concerned about the rent. I don't really want to increase my overhead."

Not saying a word, she pulled out the blueprint and pointed to where his office would be. He could see it on the ground floor, right at the front of the building. She let the silence hang in the air, then said, "The entire building is yours to access, and you can host client events in our dining room. Two concierges will be sitting at the front to greet guests as they arrive. This will be a first-class operation, and the building will be beautiful. Would you like to go see it?"

He said, "Let's go!"

They arrived at the building, and progress had been made. Marty was pleased. The parking lot was cleared of debris, and they were laying the concrete for the street signage. Marty pulled her Lexus up close to the front door, so they didn't have to walk across the parking lot. The doors had been installed, and they were magnificent. It was like walking into an antebellum mansion. Alfredo was speechless. From the blueprints, he had no idea what the exterior looked like or what her vision for the interior was, but she had done a remarkable job.

They walked over to the space that would be dedicated to his practice. She reminded him, "Alfredo, you can build out the space however you want, and you can see there is plenty of room for your secretary, and you will have access to the boardroom and our gourmet kitchen. Oh, and one more benefit, you get two private parking spaces at the back of the building."

She shared her vision for an annual Christmas party that would include all the businesses and allow them to invite their clients. She planned to use the entire first floor, including the large kitchen and dining area, for the party.

"What technology will be available?"

"The whole building will have Wi-Fi, and it is included with your rent.

"Will I have access after-hours? If a client visits after 5 o'clock, can they get in? I really need to be able to come and go at my own pace."

Marty assured him, "We are installing a keypad, and everyone will have a private code to enter the building. This will also allow us to monitor the front door if necessary. The individual offices will be left up to the occupant. Personally, I like keypad locks, but you can choose any type."

Alfredo said, "I guess the only thing I would have to change is my address, which would be easy. My secretary lives just around the corner, so she would be happy. I could do a mass-mailing to all my clients and promote an open house."

"Alfredo, that's a great idea, and don't forget that we will have two concierges at the front door with a full bar behind them. Their duty will be to greet your clients and make them feel at home. Every morning, they will brew fresh coffee, which will provide a nice aroma."

Alfredo was so excited he could hardly talk. He was overwhelmed by the possibilities. The building and space were 100% better than where he was, and teaming up with other financial professionals would be a real coup. He grasped Marty's vision, and he liked it.

"Let me think it over, I need to put a pencil to paper and figure out the logistics. I'll get back to you soon. Thanks, Marty, for thinking of me and for your time."

They shook hands and parted. The ball was now in his court, but Marty felt certain he would sign the contract and move in.

Her plan was almost complete. She only needed two more stockbrokers to complete her office. She had Heidi Becker ready to go. Marty had her attorney draw up a contract to protect her and hold her harmless for any lawsuits or damages from Heidi and any other brokers.

Now she needed to go through the stack of business cards she had collected at Linda Newkirk's party. Upon initial review, there were about fifty cards representing stockbrokers, CPAs, and financial planners. She didn't think a financial planner would work in her environment, so she ruled them out. She wanted brokers, just like her, who already had a book of clients. She could offer them a handsome commission and virtually no overhead.

She combed through the cards and picked ten to start with. She had to meet them face-to-face, so she needed to set up appointments. Getting the right mix was too important to do over the phone.

Marty started with Eric Feinstein. He was an Edward Jones broker who worked south of Dallas and could probably beat his noncompete radius clause. He was at least thirty minutes away. Edward Jones usually included a twenty-mile radius clause that protected it from anyone in its jurisdiction opening an office near its own. Brad Weddel had run into this problem when he moved to the bank, because Mesquite was only fifteen minutes from Forney. Marty learned a good lesson from that.

She called Eric and reminded him that she had met him at Linda Newkirk's party. "I would like to set up a meeting. Can you drop by my office? I have an exciting proposition to share with you. I know you're busy, so I won't take up much of your time."

He didn't appear to remember Marty, but she wasn't concerned; he would never forget her after this visit. Unfortunately for him he told her he didn't have any time and wasn't interested in what she was selling. He told her to have a good day and hung up.

Marty said to herself, "NEXT!"

She thought it made sense to look for an office with two brokers. Maybe a husband-and-wife team. She started rummaging through the cards to see if any of the last names matched. She noticed a Mary and Charles Dolly who were with Merrill Lynch. Marty thought they might be tough to pull away since Merrill Lynch was doing a lot of underwriting and IPOs. Marty's broker-dealer, Raymond James, did some, but it was mostly private placement.

However, if it worked, she could kill two birds with one stone. She decided to start with Mary. Marty got her sales assistant, who said Mary was away from her desk and offered to take a message.

Marty left her name and cell phone number. "Let her know that Marty Bledsoe called with Bledsoe and Associates, and I have something very important to discuss." That was the first time she had used the firm's name, and it felt good to say it out loud finally.

Marty remembered meeting them at the party; they were in their mid-forties. When she met them, she had imagined they both had a nice book of clients. She was really going to have to strategize to pull this couple away from Merrill Lynch. She felt certain their clients would transfer to Raymond James. Everything would be the same, except for the name on the statement. Marty felt her best approach would be negotiating an aggressive revenue-sharing plan to get them to move their books. If these two had the business that she thought they had, she would be making a wise investment.

Marty's cell phone rang, and when she answered, the voice on the other end said, "This is Mary Dolly. You left a message with my assistant. How can I be of help?"

"We met at Linda Newkirk's, and you thought it odd when I asked for your business card. You mentioned it was the first party where anyone had exchanged business cards. Do you and your husband work in the same office?"

Mary responded affirmatively and seemed curious about the call.

"I know it is none of my business, but how long have you been a broker?"

"Twenty-five years, what is it you are after?"

I have a business proposal for the two of you that could be very lucrative. I would love to treat you and Charles to dinner. How about Lawry's Prime Rib on Wednesday at six?"

Mary knew Lawry's wasn't as busy midweek, and they could talk freely. It was an excellent location with the feel of an old Chicago steakhouse. Marty always thought there was probably a mob boss or two in the crowd. Their prime rib was the best in town. She planned to wine and dine them and then tell them about the building and her business plan. They officed in the Galleria, so Lawry's was right across the tollway.

To Marty's surprise, Mary said, "It's a date, but let me double-check with Charles to make sure."

After giving it some thought, Marty felt that since the Galleria was 45 minutes from Mesquite, their clientele would be completely different. She didn't think they would be a good fit and didn't want to waste either of their time. Marty called Mary's assistant and let her know that something had come up and she needed to cancel their dinner.

She decided it would be best to look for bank reps. Her offer would be a step up for them, and they could build their own book of business, which they are not allowed to do at a bank. The banks owned their brokerage customers. However, that didn't mean those customers couldn't be moved, which would be the key in luring them to her concept.

She needed bank reps who could move a lot of accounts and wondered whether any banks were undergoing reorganization. If so, they would have the best candidates, because the volatility left employees uncertain about their futures. Mergers and acquisitions in the banking world were not favorable for a brokerage. There was always too much overlap, and they had to lay off employees.

Marty pulled out the business card for Emily Newman, a broker at Wells Fargo in the Mesquite branch downtown. Marty remembered spending a lot of time talking to her at Linda's party. She told Marty that she was one of their top producers, and Marty had been impressed by how well-dressed she was and the way she carried herself. The only downside was that she was in her early 30s, but she wasn't bouncy or perky.

She seemed to be very serious about what she was doing, and she didn't overdrink. That was a good sign. It was amazing how many brokers got plastered just because the alcohol was free. Marty always felt that at professional gatherings, people should act like gentlemen and ladies.

Marty called Emily, and she answered. She sounded very professional, and Marty got right to the point. “Emily, this is Marty Bledsoe. We met and spent time talking at Linda Newkirk’s.”

“Yes, Marty, I really enjoyed our visit. What can I do for you?”

“I have a business proposal I would like to discuss, but it would be best to do so away from the bank. Would you be interested in meeting for lunch?”

“Sure, I’m free tomorrow if that works for you.”

“That would be great.”

“There is a barbecue restaurant close to the bank. They get busy, so we might want to meet right when they open at eleven.”

Immediately upon arrival, they placed their orders and grabbed a seat. Marty brought her attaché, of course, and no purse. Emily carried a satchel, and Marty wondered what was in it. Did she carry lipstick, too?

Marty got right to the point, “Emily, I’m opening my own OSJ and wondered if you would be interested in moving as an independent. We are a full-service house backed by the broker-dealer, Raymond James. I’m the firm’s principal and hold a Series 24 license, which allows me to manage brokers. We are finishing construction on a new building, and I am looking for two sharp brokers to round out our branch.”

Emily was in a corporate environment and unfamiliar with what an independent advisor would do.

“It would be like owning your own business where you own the clients, and earn a nice commission generated from the business that you do with them. Are you earning a commission now?”

Emily responded, “No, Wells Fargo is against paying commissions because they feel the brokers will be too aggressive. They pay me a salary of $24,000 per year. I’ve been with the bank for a little over three years and have made a lot of relationships. In fact, I have won many awards for opening new accounts.”

“How do you get your new accounts—referrals from the FSRs?”

"Many just walk up to my desk."

"Do you have your insurance license?" Marty wondered what kind of investments she was familiar with. What were her mutual fund choices?

Emily said, "No, the bank doesn't handle any investments that require that kind of license." "Would you consider getting an insurance license? You could offer variable annuities."

"Sure."

"Emily, I must be frank. If you can't get your license, that would be a deal breaker for me."

"I don't think it would be too hard, but I'm not sure how I could secure it without the bank knowing."

Marty had a feeling that she was right for the position. She felt Emily could bring a bunch of clients from the bank and start her own book. Banks gave terrible service and had very limited access to financial investments. The environment at the Wells Fargo branch in Mesquite was cold and sterile. Emily had told her that she had her own office, but did not have a secretary or anyone to answer her phone. She felt like a side item at the bank, that if they could earn some fee income from her, then great, but that wasn't their primary business.

Marty knew this was the reason for the tremendous turnover in banks' brokerage systems. Banks did not understand how to treat stockbrokers, which was a good thing for Marty. Emily had taken extensive notes during their lunch, and Marty liked that. It meant she was paying attention and was interested. Plus, she could read back over them later after the meeting.

"Emily, I think you can make a lot of money and build a huge clientele if you are willing to work hard."

Emily responded, "I have a list of all the customer accounts from the bank with over $10,000 in deposits. I also have all the CD information, which includes the amounts and maturity dates."

"Going after those could be a tad unethical. You will probably want to start with the customers you are working with rather than approach other bank customers. Well, we are getting a little ahead of ourselves."

Marty had decided she was willing to take a chance on Emily, so she gave her the address of The Ivy House and let her know it was still under construction.

"Please drive by and see if you could envision yourself working independently alongside other successful people. When it is finished, you could have your own office and a sales assistant. We are putting together a one-stop shop that will include a CPA firm, Farmers Insurance Agency, and other financial service professionals. You might be a perfect fit, but you will have to work hard on the phone."

They ended the luncheon with a handshake, and Marty was impressed with her grip. They had discussed a lot, and there was still a lot on the table. Marty wanted to offer her a job, but she wanted Emily to drive by The Ivy House first. It would test her level of interest. If she could envision herself in an office among all the other successful people, she would fit in perfectly. Marty would wait to hear from her and continue her search for one more broker.

After meeting with Emily, Marty hadn't really thought about it, but she decided she would like a staff of all women financial advisors. Women's power!

Next on her list was Martha Cunningham, another woman she met at Linda's party. She was with Bank of America in an office in North Dallas, which could create a distance issue. Or it might work if Martha didn't want to fight traffic anymore and preferred to live in the suburbs. Marty remembered her as a robust, jolly person. She thought she would be a lot of fun to go out and party with.

The Bank of America platform was very different from Wells Fargo's. They had merged with Merrill Lynch, and as a result, their platform changed overnight. They were much more aggressive in the financial services sector, which is where Marty was looking to recruit. She had heard that their advisers earned a commission in addition to their base pay. She could offer the same if she had to. Every deal could be different, because each representative was different. Marty would do whatever it took to get the right person in her branch.

Marty called her but was intercepted by Martha's sales assistant, Stephanie, who told her Martha was on another call and that she should be finished in just a minute if she'd like to hold. "Yes," Marty stated with determination.

When Martha finally answered the phone, Marty told her they had met at Linda Newkirk's party and that she would be in the Galleria the next day and would love to meet for lunch.

"There is a wonderful Chinese restaurant named Asa in the Galleria that would be perfect for a power lunch. It's named after its founder, Asa Ming."

Martha said, "Sounds like a grand idea."

Marty didn't give her any information about the intention of her meeting. She wanted to hear about her practice and find out where she was in her office before discussing her plans. She couldn't wait to find out what part of town she lived in. The traffic in North Dallas was horrendous. It was much easier to drive to the suburbs than to the heart of Dallas. Normal driving time was an hour from whichever direction you were coming.

Marty planned to allow herself an hour and a half since she was driving from Mesquite. Marty smiled to herself, "Heaven forbid I get there early and have to shop."

Marty valet-parked and walked into the Galleria Mall. It was always such a pleasure to be there. The mall was full of high-end merchandise. Nordstrom's was one of their anchor stores, and they were known for their impeccable *Old School* customer service. Marty loved the store and was determined to shop even if she had to go after her appointment. Marty had already called her personal shopper to let her know she would be stopping by. She knew Marty's taste and would pull items for her to look at before her arrival. Marty knew she wouldn't be able to leave there without spending at least $500.

Entering Asa, she was reminded of its seductive environment with low candlelight and white starched tablecloths. The waitstaff wore all black. It was a first-class restaurant, and the food was delicious. Marty had been there many times when she worked for Personnel Connection. In fact, she knew every inch of the mall.

The hostess greeted Marty and asked her where she would like to sit. Marty pointed to a table in the corner, out of the way and more intimate. She wanted a location where their conversation would be private and wanted Martha to feel valued and to get a sense of how Marty cared about her brokers. Maybe one day she would like to be one.

Martha arrived, and after being seated, the two of them looked over the menus and made their choices. Small talk and trivial chatter ensued, but Marty wasn't there for that. She looked at Martha and handed her a business card that read "Bledsoe and Associates."

"How would you like to be one of my associates?"

Marty had never jumped headlong into offering a job, but the building was nearing completion, and she needed to fill it. She really had nothing to lose; all Martha could say was either yes or no.

Martha was intrigued and immediately fired off a barrage of questions. Where was the office located? Who is the broker-dealer? What was the commission split? Were they limited in products? How many brokers were working out of her office? She then waited patiently for Marty to answer her questions.

"We can do everything Merrill Lynch can do and then some. We are a full-service brokerage and clear through Raymond James. I have a revenue-sharing plan for my brokers. Where do you live?"

"I'm in the Garland area."

Marty smiled and said, "You are only about 20 minutes from our building and no traffic."

She pulled out the blueprint and pointed, "Here is where your office will be located, and this is where your licensed sales assistant will be. The building is 10,000 square feet, and there will be a Farmers Insurance Agency and a CPA office. I'm looking for three experienced financial advisors who understand the importance of knowing their customers. We cover your overhead and provide state-of-the-art technology and phone system. All the brokers will be on the mezzanine level, and two concierges will greet people at the front door. We have a huge boardroom and a large gourmet kitchen where we can have lunch together and entertain clients."

She told Martha about Tim's restaurant experience and that he would be dropping in periodically to fix lunch.

"We will be like one big happy family with no competition between brokers. Your contract will strictly protect all clients. Speaking of a contract, you will be required to sign a noncompete with a 30-mile radius clause."

As Martha was digesting all the information Marty asked, "What are you getting at Bank of America?"

"They pay me a base salary of $30,000 plus a 5% override. I'm not really happy with it, and after our merger with Merrill Lynch, we have been in a constant state of flux—it's a big mess. Frankly, this opportunity couldn't have come at a better time."

She went on to say that she had grown her customer base to almost 300 clients, and they had no allegiance to the bank or Merrill.

"I can take all of them with me; they would follow me to the moon if necessary."

"I'll offer you 40% and no overhead."

"Sounds enticing, but I would really like to drive to the building, see where it is located and how it looks before I commit."

After giving her the address, Marty said, "I'll be eager to hear back from you. By the way, if you accept the position, we will have all women brokers. How fun would that be?"

Emily Newman called Marty to let her know she was in. "I'm ready to exit Wells Fargo and move into your building. I have no problem taking the insurance test and am certain I will pass. I will go ahead and order the materials at my expense and start studying."

"That sounds wonderful. Emily, we have a deal."

She let her know that the building was about a month from completion, so Emily would only have to stay another month. During that time, she should try to gather all the information she could to help her build her own business. She needed clients, and she had the perfect resources to cultivate relationships and move their business over to Bledsoe and Associates. As soon as the building was finished, they could process her paperwork and transfer her license.

She advised her, "Do not say anything to anybody at the bank. If they think you are out looking, they might let you go. I'll touch base mid-month to update you on the building. Give me a call anytime, and we can grab lunch. We have to eat, and what better way to get to know each other?"

Now Marty had three brokers, all strong women. They were going to make a lot of money together and have fun doing it.

Martha Cunningham called with another question, "From where I live in Garland, I'm only 10 minutes from the building, so the location is great, but I'm wondering how I will be able to service my clients living in North Dallas. What are your thoughts?"

"It really depends on your relationship with your clients. Do they depend on you, or would they be satisfied with any old rep?"

Martha said, "They definitely depend on me, and my relationships are strong. It would probably require me to be out of the office a lot. I need to meet them closer to their homes and businesses in North Dallas. Would that be a problem?"

"Martha, I don't see that as being a problem. Think about it from the perspective of owning your own business. Surely you wouldn't mind driving to see your clients?"

That had been the deciding factor in Martha's decision to move to Bledsoe and Associates. There were plenty of restaurants near her clients where she could meet them, and her clients liked to eat. Some preferred to meet in their homes. She had never made much commission through Bank of America because they were constantly changing the platform and goals. She was sick of the upper management and all the confusion the Merrill Lynch merger caused. Never in her wildest dreams did she think she would own her own practice, but with Marty's backing, she could make it happen. She felt it was time she opened her own practice. She was going to accept Marty's offer.

She called Marty, "I've decided to take the plunge and move my business over to Bledsoe and Associates."

"I'm so happy for you. Let me say how proud I am of your bravery because I know this is a big step and a whole different environment from the bank."

Marty was confident she would double her income in her first year of practice. Martha would need to expand her book by getting referrals from her current clients, but she was committed to them and very knowledgeable about the financial world. The work environment would accommodate her needs, and she would have access to a sales assistant and a boardroom.

When Martha visited the building, she was impressed by its size and location. She was very happy with her decision. As soon as the building was finished, she planned to move her book, which would require a lot of paperwork. She would need to fill out new account forms and transfer paperwork, but she was up to the task. In her mind, she was making a very smart decision to leave Bank of America. It was now or never.

Marty met with the building contractors, and everybody was on the same page. The building would be finished within a week, and they could move in. She now had to decide the best way to leave the bank. She wanted to exit graciously.

She would speak to Robert Halsey, after all, he was the one who hired her and saw how she grew the department beyond his expectations. She had made a considerable contribution to the bank's bottom line by bringing in the income that far surpassed what he thought she could do. Her department was bringing in as much as a bank branch.

Marty sat down and wrote a personal letter to Robert Halsey, thanking him for his support over the years. She thanked him for giving her a chance and telling her that she was very capable of building the department. She remembered that on one of their trips to East Texas, he told her he had hired her because of her ability.

She had brought over 250 accounts with her when she came to the bank and was going to ask for their release. A good portion of them were her own family. She didn't think she would have any problem with the noncompete given the income she had generated for the bank. She would let Robert know that she would steer clear of the bank's business and leave a legacy.

Marty asked her secretary, Jennifer Horn, to be in her office the next morning at 10 a.m. and asked her to bring her steno pad. She was going to compile a list of accomplishments from her time at the bank. Jennifer definitely knew something was up with Marty. She was rarely in the bank and pretty much handled her business over the phone. Brad Weddel had stepped in and taken over Marty's book and was doing a fabulous job. The clients liked him, and the bank employees liked him. He received referrals from the FSRs and was covering a couple of other branches. This was the perfect time for her to exit.

She met with Jennifer the following morning and asked her to make a list of the following: 13,000 accounts, 13 licensed brokers, three licensed sales assistants, $250 million under management, no trading errors, and that they had never filed a claim under their Errors and Omissions insurance (Marty had trained her brokers well; they were meticulous in their trading). She also had her include that they had exceeded $100,000 in fee income per month and that the quarterly trailers that came in automatically amounted to about $25,000.

She wanted to emphasize that she had built an empire of recurring income. When Jennifer finished typing the list, Marty went to Robert's secretary and made an appointment to see him. She asked her to carve out an hour. Her secretary said he was available the next day at 10 a.m.

The day had finally arrived to say goodbye to the bank. It was bittersweet. She had met so many wonderful people, and they were all good, down-to-earth, God-fearing people. They were like a big family. But it was time for her to say goodbye. She knew her future was bright, and that kept her spirits up.

She arrived at the bank at 9:45. She didn't want any lag time waiting in the office before meeting Robert. That would be agony. She walked up to his secretary's desk, and she told her to go right in. Robert had his head down, reviewing some numbers about the bank.

As she entered his office, he looked up at her with a sad look and said, "Marty, I know you are here to put in your resignation. I've felt for several months that your heart wasn't with us anymore. What are we going to do without you?

Marty set the statistics Jennifer had typed down in front of him. She reviewed the information showing everything she had accomplished, building from zero assets under management to $250 million, which was the size of the whole bank when she came to work for them. They now had a capable staff of licensed stockbrokers, and she had trained them well. Finally, the monthly income was now over six figures and growing. Robert agreed that she had done a remarkable job.

Marty assured him, “You won’t even miss me. The program is running like clockwork, and everybody is working as a team. Brad has taken over all of my accounts and is handling them like a champ. There is really no need for me to be at the Forney branch, but I do have one request.”

Robert said, “Ask me anything.”

“I would like to keep the 250 accounts I brought to the bank, most of which are my family’s. I’m opening my own practice and hiring other brokers to work under me. Please know that I will stay clear of all the bank’s customers. That would be unethical of me. I will be operating out of Mesquite and will be focusing on Dallas, not East Texas. I don’t want there to be hard feelings.”

Robert held out his hand, “I have no problem with you keeping your accounts. Marty, I want to wish you the best.”

“I appreciate your blessing. Would you mind walking with me through the lobby so I can say goodbye? Don’t you think it is important that everyone knows we are parting on good terms?”

“Absolutely.”

She was so relieved that there were no hard feelings on either side and suggested that she and Tim should have dinner with him and his wife, Sherry, soon.

The next day, Marty got the keys to her building. Bledsoe and Associates were almost ready to open their doors. The contractors had set a move-in date for Marty, so the interior designers were working to complete the interior with a mid-century décor, as Marty had requested. She had expressed a desire to use old wooden beams, which would give the building an industrial feel.

They were also overseeing the men who had been instructed about the Wi-Fi setup for the entire building to ensure the system was installed correctly. Everyone was to have access to state-of-the-art equipment and high-speed internet. They let Marty know they estimated a two-week lag between finishing the interior and the move-in date.

Her two tenants, Greg with Farmers Insurance and Alfredo Lopez, her CPA, had worked independently with the interior decorators to finish out their offices. Marty hoped they would be first-class, but she really had no say, since she had given them carte blanche to finish them however they wanted. That included their secretaries. She informed them that the overall decor was mid-century and that they wanted a consistent look. Both of them had toured the building so they knew what she meant.

Tim was active in overseeing the construction of their gourmet kitchen and dining room. He made sure that they installed all state-of-the-art appliances. He wanted to make sure that no matter how big an event was, the kitchen could accommodate it.

Marty had asked the designers to create her desk using an old door, so they placed a piece of glass on top of the door and, at either end, added wooden file cabinets the same height as the desk. In front of the desk, they placed two Queen Anne chairs for her clients. Off to the side was a table where she could sign paperwork or eat a catered lunch.

The sales assistant for the brokers also had her own office. They had installed state-of-the-art technology so she could do word processing and construct proposals. She was to answer the phone, "Bledsoe and Associates." She would send a text message when someone was out of the office. Marty wanted everyone to get back to callers within 15 minutes if possible. She also encouraged them to answer their phones when they rang and not let them go to voicemail. She let them know that even if they were in the middle of something, it was a good idea to take a break and answer the phone.

In front of the building, a marquee had been installed with Bledsoe and Associates at the top and the other businesses at the bottom. There was a scrolling sign built into the marquee that they could change daily: business names, stock symbols with prices, holiday greetings, happy birthday announcements, or whatever else the day required. She knew it would be a good way to draw the attention of people driving by. The building itself was almost welcoming enough.

Raymond James had set up a portal for her at her home office, so Marty was busy on the phone moving her accounts from the bank. Her brokers were doing the same. There was a mountain of paperwork that needed to be done, but Rome wasn't built in a day. It would take time to migrate all the accounts, but once it was done, they would be in full production.

While Marty was busy working in her office, Tim went out to the mailbox and checked the mail. He loved to walk out to the mailbox, get the mail, and see if there was anything for him. He was like a little kid at Christmas. He noticed something from the Republican National Committee. Without looking at who it was addressed to, he ripped into it. He silently wondered, "What kind of a donation are they looking for now?" They had always been very generous to the Republican Party. Tim and Marty both believed in lower taxes and less government, and that's what the party represented to them.

The letter enclosed was addressed to Mrs. Marty Bledsoe. Tim continued to read the letter. It was from the head of the Republican National Committee, Rona McDaniels. Tim could hardly believe his eyes. They had named Marty Businesswoman of the Year for Texas. They wanted to fly her and two guests to Washington so she could receive the award at a black-tie event. President Bush would be in attendance.

Tim decided not to tell Marty right away, but wanted to wait for the perfect time. He thought it would be best to tell her on the day the building opened. That would provide some additional good news on her special day.

One of the interior designers called, "Marty, would you like us to place all your awards on the walls of your office?"

One wall was all glass overlooking the lobby, and behind her desk was a wall with a credenza in front, leaving plenty of space for plaques and awards. To the right of her desk was a big open wall, but she hadn't decided what should go there. She suggested a nice big piece of art.

Tim overheard her talking and said he had to run to the building and check on something. He wanted to make sure the wall to the right of her desk was not used. That's where he planned to hang her plaque for the Businesswoman of the Year award. Upon arrival, he spoke to her designer and asked her to have one of the contractors install a spotlight to highlight the plaque.

Marty continued working with her clients and completing paperwork. She made multiple appointments to see them face-to-face; she was a big fan of in-person visits. She had the time and wanted to explain to them in person what to expect from Bledsoe and Associates in the future. She also would need their signatures on everything, so she brought her attaché and completed one transfer after another.

If there was no need for discussion, she sent her secretary to get the needed signatures. Most of her accounts were over seven figures, and she didn't plan on growing her base much more than what she already had. She would hand-select which referrals she would make to the other consultants. She no longer wanted to manage a big book.

Marty joined the Mesquite Chamber of Commerce and wanted to invite them to the open house. Marty planned to attend the Chamber lunches each month and become part of the community, and wanted the other financial advisors to do the same.

The president of the chamber was Priscilla Preston, a woman. She was a real estate mogul and was well known around the region. Marty thought she should make an appointment to visit her in person, so she called Priscilla and set up a time to go by her office.

Priscilla was happy to accommodate the appointment and said she was looking forward to meeting. "I heard you had bought and were renovating a building. I've been driving by on occasion to monitor the progress, and I must say, I am very impressed."

She had also heard that Marty was a powerhouse broker who owned her own brokerage, Bledsoe and Associates. Mesquite was a small suburb of Dallas, and there wasn't a lot happening out there, especially for women. It was still more of an East Texas environment where men were dominant.

Marty called Ken Miller and Alfredo Lopez to discuss joining the chamber. "I would really like for you to join the Mesquite Chamber; it is only $150 per year. I'm going to invite Priscilla Preston, the Chamber's President, to our open house and encourage her to ask the mayor to attend. We want all the key people in Mesquite to attend our ribbon cutting."

It was a big deal for Marty, and she intended to extend an invitation to all the community's important leaders.

They both agreed to sign up under Bledsoe and Associates. She said it would be a good look for all of them to sit at the same table at the chamber functions. She provided them with Priscilla's contact information so they could call her directly.

She also let Ken and Alfredo know that her decorators were almost finished, so they needed to move their furniture in. She wanted their offices completed at the same time as hers so that she could schedule a ribbon-cutting with the chamber.

She was still considering hosting a separate open house for clients. It would be an evening event, on a much larger scale, starting at 5 o'clock. Maybe she would serve caviar, and definitely plenty of shrimp. There would be a buffet table full of food and a champagne fountain.

Marty didn't think the building would be complete without a large American flag, so she called the contractor and asked him to install a flagpole next to the marquee and install lights to illuminate it so it could be flown at night. She wanted a big flag and a big pole. She was a true-blue American and wanted to show the world that she supported her country.

The contractor responded, "There won't be a problem illuminating the pole; we already have electricity running to the marquee. What size pole do you want?"

"At least 30 feet tall and taller if you can find one. I want it tall enough to hang a giant flag."

"That should be a good height and be balanced next to the marquee. I'll order it right away." He knew she would be mindful about how it would look, and she confirmed that's what she wanted.

Marty called Priscilla Preston at the Chamber, "I would like to plan a ribbon cutting and open house, but wanted to check with you first to see if you would be available and if so, what day would work best for you."

"I think that would be great. We can discuss dates, but you might want to give yourself plenty of time to get the word out."

Marty asked whether she would be willing to send invitations to the mayor and any other city dignitaries she thought might like to attend. Priscilla let her know that she would personally invite everyone she could think of.

They decided on a Wednesday afternoon several weeks away, giving Marty plenty of time to send out invitations and for Priscilla to spread the word. They both agreed that a strong showing of locals was necessary, given that the building itself and the renovation were impressive and beneficial for the city.

Of course, for Marty, the whole process was to get new clients. It was one thing to put on a good show, but another entirely to capture business. She was certain they would glean new clients.

The stage was set for the Chamber of Commerce ribbon-cutting. They expected a large turnout and planned to have plenty of food and drinks on hand. The champagne would be flowing. Marty hired a trio of musicians to play during the open house.

The music would bring an ambience to the event and make it more inviting. She hoped people would tour the building, visit the upper floor, and the banquet area. They planned to set up the dining room table in the gourmet kitchen as a serving station. Tim was in charge of the food, and Marty was very specific that she wanted finger food that would not fall apart before you could put it in your mouth. She didn't want food all over the floor. Valet parking would be available for all distinguished guests. She invited the local newspaper to attend and cover the event. She wanted as much free press as possible.

It was time to bring her entire team together, so she planned a luncheon. All financial advisors, concierges, sales assistants, and tenants would meet for lunch in the back room of a local restaurant to ensure privacy. The lunch was mandatory.

Marty was ready to unveil the printed marketing brochures and hand out business cards. Even the concierges and sales assistants would have business cards. She had custom gold-embossed stationery made. She was excited to discuss the grand opening plans.

"This is the beginning. We are getting ready to open for business. It must be perfect. We all need to look professional and put on a good front. Men, please wear suits with starched white shirts; women, please do not wear dangling earrings."

"I was planning for the ribbon cutting to be a preview of the building and then host a much more upscale open house just for clients. We are not sure what kind of crowd will attend. What are your thoughts?"

They openly discussed and felt that hosting a second event would honor their clients and would be a great way to get them to visit the new space. Marty suggested they send out personal invitations to each client, addressed by hand. Everyone agreed. She informed them of the Wednesday date she had set with the Chamber of Commerce for the ribbon-cutting and asked everyone to clear their calendars for that day.

"No client visits on that day; all of our focus needs to be directed toward our clients and visitors from the city. There will be no drinking by any of us. I would prefer not to have alcohol, but that's not a good idea at an opening. We will let the guests drink as much as they want, but we are not to imbibe."

They were ready to open the building doors, and the entire staff was ready. All the furniture was in, the lights were turned on, and the computers were running at full speed.

The day finally arrived for the ribbon-cutting with the Chamber of Commerce. Priscilla Preston arrived thirty minutes early to tour the building and review the work completed. All the food was prepared and laid out to entice the visitors to eat and sip champagne. Priscilla said to expect a lot of the town's business owners. She said she had never been to a business so beautiful and compelling.

She pulled Marty aside and told her she wanted to discuss moving her business over to Marty. This would definitely be an account Marty would handle. The referrals that she could bring would be unlimited. Priscilla knew everybody in Mesquite and the surrounding suburbs. Marty would take special care of her, just like she did with all of her clients. Marty was seeking new clients, and planning this event proved to be a great way to generate business in the town.

A balloon canopy draped over the front door signaled a party inside. The dignitaries and business owners began to arrive on time. Soon, there was a backup at the valet station, so people started parking their own cars. It wasn't that long of a walk to the front door anyway.

Clients and visitors streamed in, and the building was a big hit. Everybody admired the renovation and loved the decor. It was an environment that smelled of money.

Everyone was having a great time, and the background music added an elegant ambience. Marty had planned this day to be unlike any other grand-opening ribbon-cutting; it was intended to be a full-blown party. She hoped everyone enjoyed the champagne and hors-d'oeuvres. Most chamber events were designed to foster networking and generate more business for members. This was not designed as a networking environment; it was meant to be fun. However, Marty, not being one to miss a networking opportunity, set up a large fish-bowl at one of the concierge desks with a sign reading, "Drop your business card and one lucky winner will win an Apple iPad."

The fishbowl was a big hit — everybody put their cards in. She planned to distribute the cards to her people so they could follow up with everyone later. It was her idea to make it a warm call rather than a cold call.

The mayor finally arrived, and the party was full steam ahead. The mayor told Marty, "I don't think I have ever been to an event so posh. There are very few women business owners in Mesquite. I want you to know how proud I am of you. I'm looking forward to the ribbon-cutting."

He introduced her to several business owners, then excused himself, saying, "I think I'll have a little champagne and sample the hors d'oeuvres."

Tim had not yet told Marty about the letter from the Republican National Committee naming her the businesswoman of the year for Texas. He thought announcing the award at the client's open house would honor her the most. He was eager to share the news with her but decided to wait for the most opportune time.

Eventually, the event began to wind down, and everyone started to leave. You could definitely tell there was a party in the building. Marty felt it was a success, and the fishbowl was filled with business cards. Tim said the hors d'oeuvres were a big hit, and they were almost out of food. He had a cleanup crew ready to restore the building to business-ready condition.

Everyone was starting to get back to business. They were there to make money, not just sit idle. The transfers for all the advisers were happening at a rapid pace. The sales assistants were doing a great job of processing paperwork quickly and sending it to the corporate office. Ray Willis, from Raymond James, checked in on Marty frequently. He was monitoring the process and ensuring everything worked perfectly for her. She was bringing significant business to them, and he wanted to provide her with the best possible service.

Marty decided to use some of her bonus money to reimburse her clients for the fees that came with transferring their accounts. Usually, when an IRA was transferred, a closeout fee would be incurred from the other firm.

Marty wanted Pacific Life, a large insurance company, to train the advisers on variable life insurance. It was a brand-new product for all of them, and there were many details. There were significant benefits for clients, especially high-net-worth clients, with whole life insurance. Pacific Life thought it best to have them come to their corporate offices in Las Colinas for training.

They suggested a four-hour training class for each advisor. This was a highly complex investment and required extensive research by the advisor to determine its appropriateness. Marty was the first to go to Pacific Life's Corporate office for the training. She wanted to make sure it was the right investment before committing to the many hours of training required.

Marty drove to Las Colinas to their corporate offices. They were in a tall, modern, chic glass building. "This is not your normal insurance company," thought Marty. They had an AAA rating, and the mutual fund families inside the investment were all familiar to Marty. The looming question, "What is the benefit to our clients?"

Insurance was not at the top of her leaderboard. She found it boring, except for variable annuities. They were wrapped in life insurance but were essentially tax shelters, similar to an IRA. The caveat was that if the beneficiary was different than your spouse, there could be a tax issue from the distribution. With the variable life investment, no taxes were due to the beneficiaries.

Nathan Redding, the Pacific Life representative selected to train Marty, met her in the lobby and escorted her to their computer training room. He offered her a cold drink or bottled water; she chose bottled water. He seated her at a terminal and activated the mouse—the Pacific Life logo appeared. There were icons across the bottom of the screen for various commands.

Nathan asked her to click on the proposal icon. The form that appeared was quite complicated. A substantial amount of information had to be gathered to draft the contract, and the client needed to be in relatively good health. Marty thought to herself, "This could be an investment that she could spend weeks on processing and be turned down due to a client's health."

She brought three of her client profiles to the training. Nathan wanted her to be able to generate proposals based on real-life situations. She started with the Stewarts, who were both retired and had a mountain of cash in their tax-free money market. Nathan said the product would be based solely on one person's life, so Marty chose the elder of the two.

They entered numbers and dates, completed the template, and generated a proposal. Their death benefit would be $1 million, but they had to invest a set amount for five years to pay the premium. Nathan said they could withdraw from the policy at any time once the insurance was paid up, and any withdrawal would be tax-free. The most important consideration was that the benefit would pass tax-free to their children. Over the life of the investment, Marty could manage the mutual funds in their portfolio to achieve their objectives, whether they wanted growth and income, growth, or just income.

They worked through the other two clients that Marty had brought, and she was starting to get a feel for how the proposal program worked. Several variables determined the premium and death benefit. Her job was to invest in the mutual funds inside the variable life contract. She saw their product as an excellent option that would deliver substantial value to her book of business.

She closed out the training session by saying, "I believe we will be able to draft many contracts—we will be proud to represent Pacific Life. I plan to send my advisers for the same training, and I'm sure they will come away feeling positive about your product, as well."

Her sales assistant called to request the final details regarding the invitations for the upcoming client open house. She had prepared a rendition and needed Marty's input and approval. Marty told her she would be back in the office in the afternoon, and they could go over them then.

They had set a deadline to get out the invitations in plenty of time for clients to respond. On the outside of the invitation, Bledsoe and Associates was to be written in gold. She wanted the inside of the envelope in gold, too. She wanted it to feel regal, and it had to match their stationery.

Each advisor and tenant received fifty invitations. They were to invite their very best clients. Marty's theory was that your best clients would refer them to the best clients. Even though the mayor and Priscilla Preston had attended the public open house, she wanted them there so she could introduce them to their clientele. She planned to ask the mayor to say a few words about the building and what it meant to Mesquite that Bledsoe and Associates were there. She would also invite some of the city council members. She intended to hand-address the invitations to the mayor, Priscilla, and several city council members.

They began setting the stage for a night of glitz and glamour. A photo booth was set up for pictures with the dignitaries. A baby grand piano was brought into the lobby for the music. Marty surprised everyone by telling them that she had purchased the piano and planned for it to take up permanent residence in the lobby to be used for future events. She played the piano and loved the acoustics of the building.

Tim oversaw the caterers, servers, and bartenders. He planned for the servers to be dressed in white tuxedos with white gloves. They would be instructed to mingle through the crowd, carrying silver platters laden with various finger foods. He hired two bartenders to man the bars, where the clients could order a double martini shaken, not stirred.

Marty and Tim decided to start planning what they would wear to the gala. Marty wanted to go to Highland Park Village and the Chanel store to find a tea-length pale pink gown. Tim wanted to shop at Hermès for a suit that would fit the occasion. Maybe he would add a pocket square. So, they headed to the Village to shop, and while they were there, they stopped at Café Pacific, their favorite restaurant in Dallas, for lunch and dirty martinis.

They walked into the Chanel store and were greeted by a salesclerk. "Ma'am, is there anything in particular you are looking for?"

In true Marty fashion, she said confidently, "Of course, eveningwear, a cocktail style dress, something in pale pink."

The salesclerk pointed to the front window and said, "Something like that?" The color was a perfect pale pink, off-the-shoulder gown with a black crinoline. She thought it would look great with rhinestone-covered shoes. She quickly tried on the gown and wanted Tim's approval. He was across the parking lot at Hermès shopping on his own. The salesclerks were busy pinning and tucking where the gown needed altering. She texted Tim, asking him to come right away. He said he would be right there.

Tim gasped when he saw Marty, "You look like a fairy princess, pink is definitely your color. The dress is perfect." He looked at one of the salesclerks, "We'll take it."

Marty wondered how he had fared, and he said, "Let's finish up here and walk over so I can show you some of the suits we picked out."

The day had finally arrived for the client's open house. RSVPs had come flooding in, so they were expecting a big crowd. The mayor of Mesquite planned to attend, along with several city council members. Everything was set for a fabulous evening of music and laughter. Marty was hopeful that the event would generate many referrals.

The event was set to start at 5 P.M., so Marty let everybody go after lunch. She wanted to give them plenty of time to get ready. They were to wear cocktail attire. She told them she had bought a dress in Highland Park and that Tim had bought a new suit. They were both going to be overdressed, but this was a special occasion. The other consultants said they had also bought new dresses. Everyone was so excited and couldn't wait for the party to begin.

The building renovation was perfect. Flowers were placed all over the lobby and the mezzanine level, and there were candles in all the nooks and crannies. The waiters were ready in their white gloves with silver trays loaded with finger sandwiches and small bite-sized hors d'oeuvres.

The Mayor, Tom O'Malley, was the first to arrive, and he was early. He told a waiter he needed to speak with Tim, and the waiter went to the kitchen, where Tim was ensuring everything was being prepared correctly. When he emerged from his haven, the Mayor said, "Tim, I have a special gift for Marty, and I need you to hide it for me. I would prefer you pick a place close to where I will be speaking."

Tim found the perfect spot under the stairwell and instructed one of the waitstaff to ensure the present was delivered when Marty introduced him and the council members in attendance.

The guests started arriving in droves. Marty hoped all her clients would attend. They had been with her for years, and this was a big step for her. She was very proud to show them the building and introduce them to her other consultants.

Marty wanted to greet everyone, so she stood at the front door and shook hands with guests as they arrived, and encouraged them to enjoy the party. Also, the pianist greeted them at the baby grand piano, playing the music Marty had selected, which was upbeat and recognizable.

She had deliberately positioned her consultants in strategic locations throughout the first floor. She wanted them to offer building tours and advised them to escort guests to their own offices.

The doors to the gourmet kitchen were open, where Tim had set up a buffet table for all to enjoy. The hors d'oeuvres were being served by the waiters, but he knew you could not have too much food. The bartenders were standing guard, ready to fill orders. Marty had insisted on real glass, not plastic cups.

There was a huge turnout. Everyone was enjoying themselves, and drinks were flowing freely. Even a few people were dancing close to the grand piano. The festivities were in full swing, and the crowd was moving toward the mezzanine and beyond, into the kitchen. Everyone wanted to see the renovated building, and they were all amazed at the decor and progress. Her tenants were also having a good time, and their clientele turned out, as well. They were handing out cards to everyone, especially those people they didn't know.

Marty tried to introduce as many people as she could to the mayor and the city council members present. She wanted everyone to know that she was invested in the small suburb and the dignitaries who ruled it.

Marty was hoping they got a lot of business from the party. Marty had to find a way to distribute referrals among her consultants fairly. She planned to keep her seven-figure accounts but did not want to expand her book. She wanted her brokers to have the lion's share of the business. The sales assistants would be instructed to rotate all leads among the consultants so that everyone received their fair share. She would call the rotation, "Broker of the Day." Some major accounts would be coming in, and her team deserved the best clientele.

Once the party was in full swing, Marty got up on the stairs and clinked her champagne flute to get everybody's attention. First, she introduced her consultants, Heidi, Emily, and Martha: "These ladies are incredible advisors and are happy to meet with any of you and share their special investment knowledge. Next, I would like to introduce two of our tenants, Ken Miller with Farmers Insurance, and CPA Alfredo Lopez. Ken and Alfredo have handled our personal business for years, and they are the best at what they do. I would encourage you to introduce yourself to them and seek their counsel."

She looked over at Tim and raised her glass, "Please join me in honoring my husband, Tim Rooney. This night would not have been possible without his help. He actually bought the building for me and all of our clients.

She then introduced Mayor O'Malley and the various city council members who were present. The mayor mounted the stairs and approached her, saying he would like to say a few words. She accommodated his request and clinked his glass to get everybody's full attention. Marty thought he was going to put in a good word about the city of Mesquite, but she was wrong.

"Tonight, I have a special gift for Marty." He motioned for Tim to hand him the package that they had stored under the stairs. "On behalf of the city of Mesquite, I want to congratulate Marty for the outstanding renovation she has done on the building and what it represents for the city and this area of town. Women own less than 3% of the businesses in Mesquite. Marty, this is a little something that we would like you to have."

Tim helped her unwrap the package, and to both of their surprise, it was a large key with a big red ribbon. Mayor O'Malley said, "Marty, we offer you the key to our city. You are the first woman to ever get this award."

Marty ran up the stairs, grabbed the key, and held it up high so everybody could see it. Now she knew what she would put on the blank wall in her office.

Tim immediately spoke up and said, "What a great honor, but I have another big announcement for all of us tonight. The Republican National Committee in Washington reached out to me and said they had selected Marty as the businesswoman of the year for Texas."

The crowd erupted in applause. Marty couldn't believe her ears. She stood there as if in a time warp. She didn't know what to say or do, which was highly unusual for her because she always had something to say. Finally, she said, "I can't believe they would bestow this honor on me, but I will gladly accept it and am proud to represent Texas."

Marty closed out the evening by saying, "We want you all to know that we will be having an annual Christmas-Hanukkah party, and everyone is invited. Throughout the year, we will also host many luncheons and special events. Thank you from the bottom of my heart for attending. On your way out be sure to sign our guestbook."

# CHAPTER 9

## WASHINGTON D.C.

The problem with putting your foot on the tigers neck is you can never let up.

A large envelope arrived from the Republican National Committee, and Marty tore into it. Tim told her they were inviting her to Washington, D.C., to accept the award in person. She couldn't wait to see what the itinerary was and hoped there would be time for sightseeing. There was so much to see there.

Inside the envelope were two airline tickets, hotel reservations, and arrangements for limousine service to transport them to and from the convention center where the event was to be held. It appeared there would be plenty of time for sightseeing. There were also three passes to the event.

Marty thought it would be great to invite Ray Willis from Raymond James to accompany her and Tim, so she called him to share the good news.

"Marty, we have never had anybody in the company win an award like this. I am so proud of you."

"Ray, Tim, and I would like you to join us. We don't have an airline ticket for you, but we do have an extra pass for the event."

He laughed and said, "I accept your offer. I think Raymond James will be more than happy to pick up the tab."

He asked where they would be staying. She let him know it was being held at the Hilton across the street from the convention center.

They had about two months to plan for the trip. Lily Francis would be taking care of Ryan, so their home front was covered. They were to fly in on a Wednesday, and the event would be held on Friday evening. This meant they were free all day Thursday to use the limousine service for sightseeing. Ray wasn't flying in until Thursday night; he told Marty he wasn't much into sightseeing. Friday was reserved for meetings with their state representatives and senators. There would also be time for pictures and autographs.

On Friday evening, the award ceremony would be black-tie, so Tim decided it was time to buy a tuxedo rather than rent one. He had never owned a tuxedo, but he felt that this occasion was a good reason to pull the trigger. He called Bonnie Murphy French, his haberdasher, to come over and take his measurements. He trusted her to design something that would be different than anyone else's tux. He hoped that she would have enough time to complete it before the event.

He always used Bonnie for custom-made apparel. She had a fashionable flair and always suggested the best accessories to complement any suit or sports coat he ordered. Bonnie told him she had all his measurements but would drop by to confirm, as there are different ways to construct a tuxedo jacket. She definitely planned to trim it in satin and have a satin stripe down each leg. She suggested he buy some black patent leather slip-ons to complete the look.

Marty was set on her outfit: the pale-pink Chanel cocktail dress she had worn to the open house. Part of the itinerary required her to wear a business suit, so she chose a blue silk suit with a Valentino blouse. She would wear nude pumps, which were perfect for any occasion. Since Tim had pockets, she decided not to take a purse. He could easily carry her necessities, including her lipstick.

Ray called to ask about the itinerary, and Marty said she would email it to him.

"Do you know if there will be any photo opportunities? I would like to include some pictures in our monthly newsletter. If possible, I would like to sit up close to the stage when you accept your award."

She informed him that the schedule included time for photos and that she hoped to have her picture taken with one of the senators.

"President Bush is expected to attend, maybe we can get him to take a photo with the two of us. After all, he is from Texas. It would be great if I could get a picture while shaking his hand."

Ray called the Hilton to secure a room but was told all the regular rooms were booked. He pivoted, "Do you have a presidential suite?"

"Of course, would you like me to reserve the suite for you?"

"Yes, that's the one I want." He hoped the suite was large enough to host a reception after the event and invite many of the dignitaries and people they would meet.

The presidential suite was available at a hefty cost, but Ray thought it was worth it. What Marty was doing was very special, and he wanted to show her that Raymond James was behind her 110%. He planned to take Marty and Tim's room and let them have the presidential suite. He wasn't going to tell Marty; he wanted it to be a surprise. He hoped the whole trip would be full of surprises for her, because she certainly deserved them.

Ray called Marty back, "Well, I secured a room at the Hilton. When you and Tim check in, there will be a little surprise waiting."

Marty loved surprises. He knew they had a limousine service shuttling them around DC, so he rented a car for himself. He did not want to be a third wheel, but be there for support, nothing more. He thought to himself, "This is going to be a trip that none of them will ever forget."

Their bags were packed, and they were ready to go the next day. They packed carefully so they didn't take any unnecessary items. They strategically planned for every event, knowing what they would wear.

Marty arranged with the hotel to have a hairstylist and a makeup artist at her disposal. For the awards ceremony, she wanted her hair in a French twist. She never passed up an opportunity to look her best. She thought that all that prep would go well with the dress.

Tim called Marty at work and told her they were having a special dinner that night. "I'm taking you to Lawry's Restaurant for a prime rib dinner."

Lawry's was located in North Dallas off the tollway, one of Marty's favorite places to go. She wondered what Tim had up his sleeve. "We are leaving in the morning on the trip of a lifetime. Why else would he want to take me out?"

Marty left the office early to get ready for the special night out. Something was definitely brewing. She hoped it would arrive in a light-blue box, meaning it would be from Tiffany's. Tim was constantly showering her with jewelry. She felt like the Queen of England with the stash of jewelry he bestowed on her. Her interest was definitely piqued.

Tim had called ahead and made reservations. You never knew what the crowd would be like at Lawry's, and he wanted to make sure to secure one of their half-moon-shaped booths. He wanted plenty of room for his surprise.

They jumped in the Lexus and headed for North Dallas. When they arrived, they were seated and given menus, but Marty already knew what she wanted, the California cut of prime rib, plenty for her appetite. They had large copper carving stations strategically placed around the dining room, from which they sliced the meat and served side dishes. One of the highlights was the spinning-bowl salad, served with a chilled fork. The waiter held the dressing high and began spinning a cold silver bowl as he drizzled it over the salad. It was quite a show. They ordered red wine and watched the show.

Lawry's was known for their exquisite banana cream pie, which had to be at least seven inches tall. Marty was too full to order dessert, but Tim had his eye on the cream Brulé. Marty didn't know where he put all the food; he didn't look like an over-eater. In fact, she thought he had a great body.

As they completed their meal, the waiter began clearing the table. Marty excused herself and went to the restroom, giving Tim some time to do whatever it was he was up to. She wondered what he had in store. In the past, he mentioned buying an apartment complex, but surely that wouldn't qualify for a dinner out. That would mean meeting at their attorney's office to sign a bunch of papers. He didn't bring any packages or his briefcase, so she couldn't imagine what he had up his sleeve, but she was excited to find out.

When she got back to the table, there were three boxes on it. All had Skibell Jewelers on the side, which meant they were from her favorite jewelry store in Dallas's Highland Park Village.

Marty started with the smallest box first. It was a beautiful pink pearl-and-diamond ring. It perfectly matched her dress for the awards dinner. Then she went for the second biggest box. It was a five-strand pink pearl bracelet with a diamond clasp. Again, it matched her dress perfectly. Then she opened the last box, which was long; she guessed that it probably held a necklace. She opened it, and her eyes could not believe what she was seeing. Five strands of pink pearls with a diamond brooch on the front, a choker necklace with a diamond clasp on the back.

She loved pink pearls, and Tim had once given her a strand, but nothing like this. These would complete her outfit for the most important awards dinner of her life. She loved him so much and thanked him for the thoughtful gifts. He knew exactly what to get her; it was almost as if he could read her mind.

## THE AWARD

Tim had ORDERED a limousine to pick them up at the house and deliver them to the airport. He also upgraded their tickets to first class. If there was ever a time in their life to celebrate, this was it. Marty was unaware of any of his plans, so when Tim announced the car was ready, her mouth fell open at the sight of the black limousine in front of their house. They had packed and planned well. They were ready to jet off to the beautiful city of Washington D.C. Marty planned to take full advantage of their time together, mapping out where they would go and the events they would attend before the awards dinner.

They arrived at the airport, and as the boarding began, Tim led her to the gate. She didn't understand how they were getting to go first, but she was along for the ride. She soon learned when they were seated in first class. The stewardess immediately brought warm mixed nuts and asked for their drink order. Marty ordered Champagne, and Tim decided to join her. She was pleasantly surprised by the upgrade. She had never flown first class, and she knew that Tim was behind this great surprise.

They landed in DC, and a limo driver held a sign with their name at baggage claim. This came as no surprise, since they had been told they would have a driver while in DC. They walked over to him and pointed to their bags. He pulled them off the carousel, and they all proceeded to the car. Marty was thrilled with the attention to detail. It was first class all the way. They told the driver to take them straight to their hotel so they could unpack and have a nice dinner.

Tim went to the check-in desk and was told they had been upgraded to a different room. The clerk told him that Ray Willis was taking their room. Tim wondered what an upgrade could be, but he liked the sound of it. He knew Marty would be thrilled. The valet grabbed their bags and motioned them to an elevator at the end of the hall, separate from the others.

When they stepped off the elevator, they entered a gigantic suite on the penthouse level. A chandelier hung over a dining room table that could seat twelve. There was a large living room with a big-screen TV and a full kitchen. Marty figured the suite must have been at least three thousand square feet.

Ray had mentioned that Raymond James wanted to host a reception after the awards dinner, and Marty knew the suite was the perfect venue. All they needed was food and a bartender. Tim was excited to see the bedroom and ensuite; they were absolutely stunning. Oh, what a night they were about to have.

On the large dining room table was a huge basket filled with cheese and crackers, chocolates, and wine. Flowers had been staged around the room. Ray had done an excellent job of making their stay special. Marty noticed a letter from Ray on the table and opened it. "Marty, I hope the room suits you and Tim, and that you enjoy DC. Order anything from room service, it's on me. I'll be flying tomorrow, so let's plan to have dinner. Meet me in the lobby at 6 o'clock and ask Tim to wear a jacket. I have a special place in mind." Marty looked forward to seeing him and thanking him.

They woke up the next morning and ordered room service, planning to eat in bed. Afterward, they got ready and set off to see all the sites in Washington. First, they went to the White House and took a tour. Next was the Smithsonian Institution, then the Washington Monument, and finally the Lincoln Memorial.

They ended the day back at the Hilton in time for happy hour. They both enjoyed a dirty martini before going up to the room to get dressed for dinner. They were in the lobby at 6 o'clock waiting for Ray, who was right on time. They jumped into the limousine and headed to a famous DC restaurant where diplomats and senators liked to be seen. What a wonderful dinner it was, but Marty was almost too excited to eat. The trip was like living in a dream.

The day had finally arrived for Marty to receive her award. She woke up beaming, wondering what the day would bring. She was excited to meet people from other states and had been told that dignitaries from around the world were attending. Some of the U.S Ambassadors and other representatives would also be in attendance. The evening was set to be quite an experience, and everybody would be in black tie.

Ray called, and Tim answered, "What is a good time for me to send up a crew to set up the suite for the reception after tonight's award dinner? They will be setting up a full bar, but I don't expect it to take them very long. I've asked the hotel to provide the hors-d'oeuvres, and of course, the bartenders and servers."

"This morning really works best. I've scheduled massages for us, so give us an hour, and the suite is all theirs. Marty's glamour squad is scheduled to arrive at 2:00 to do her hair and makeup, so it would be good if they were done by then."

Tim thought her glamor session would be a good time for him to get in a long run. Afterward, Marty was scheduled to take pictures with a Texas senator. The photo booths were being set up, with the White House as a backdrop.

All the fussing over her hair, makeup, and dress was complete. Tim told her she looked beautiful. They walked across the street to the convention center, where a full-blown press squad met her. There were cameras and lots of pictures. She would treasure the photos for the rest of her life.

Ray had called earlier to make sure the room had been set up. Marty told him they had done an excellent job, with flowers everywhere. She wondered how much he had paid for this experience. She was so grateful to have his attention and support. Ray told her he had invitations printed for her to hand out at the event, and that she could invite anyone she wanted. The event was scheduled for three hours, so the invitations said the party would start at 9 P.M. The caterers were to come in and set up all the food while they were at the banquet. Ray pulled out all the stops, ordering caviar and all the accoutrements, and said the champagne would be flowing and the atmosphere would be exciting.

The awards ceremony was held at the large convention center in DC, across the street from the Hilton. Ray, Tim, and Marty met in the lobby at 4 P.M. and walked together to the center. When they entered, they saw large signs posted for each state, where everyone was supposed to register.

They walked over to the Texas table and introduced themselves. They were given a table number and told to stand in line at the entry door to the banquet room. The place was packed; people were everywhere. Marty was sure that once the doors opened, everyone would be scrambling to get to their table. As they approached the entry door, they were greeted by a Marine clad in a full-dress uniform and white gloves.

"Mrs. Bledsoe, may I have the pleasure of escorting you to your table?"

Marty looked over at Tim and Ray and gave them a wink. The marine ushered them past everyone standing in line. The room itself was elegant with large crystal chandeliers hanging from the ceiling. Marty guessed the room could hold several thousand people.

The tables were round, seating ten at each. They approached a table, and immediately knew it was theirs. The centerpiece was a Dallas Cowboys jersey, a Texas star, and bluebonnets were everywhere. White, crisp tablecloths adorned every table, with a black cloth underneath and black napkins. There were gold chargers and gold flatware with wine glasses for each course. The RNC had asked Marty to choose an entrée, so she had chosen surf and turf, knowing Tim would love it. They were the first to arrive at the Texas table, so they seated themselves facing the stage. Marty couldn't wait to meet the other attendees who would be seated at their table.

The crowd started to filter in and take their seats. As soon as someone sat at Marty's table, she got up and introduced herself. Several freshman representatives and ambassadors from various countries gathered around the Texas table. Marty had never heard of some of the countries they represented. Her geography wasn't great, but they all spoke English and knew where Dallas, Texas was. The conversations were lively, and everybody felt the excitement in the air. The lights dimmed, and the chandeliers gleamed. It was time for the program to begin.

The master of ceremonies was Newt Gingrich. He took to the podium and introduced the people at the head table on stage, "Ladies and gentlemen, we have with us tonight our President, George Bush."

Then he moved around the table, introducing all the senators and representatives and their wives. He welcomed everyone from across the United States and said those in attendance were the best of the best in business.

"As we eat dinner and break bread together, I want to encourage everybody to meet the people around you," Mr. Gingrich said.

He went on to explain that dinner would be served, and then the awards ceremony would commence.

The tables weren't in alphabetical order, so it was fun to get up and meet people from other states. The Texas table was situated at the front of the room, right under the stage. Next to it were the Alabama and California tables.

The dinner was more like a feast. The service and the food were excellent, and everybody was in a good mood. Marty made a special effort to meet everyone at the tables around her. Some of the business owners wore special name tags, and she congratulated them on their awards. Ray had brought his briefcase, full of invitations for the after-party. Marty started handing them out as the dessert was served. She hoped for a great turnout; everyone looked excited when she handed them an invitation.

Marty was ready to walk on stage, receive her award, take it back to her office, and proudly hang it on the blank wall next to her key to the city of Mesquite.

Newt Gingrich walked to the podium after all the dinner plates were cleared, "Well, it is the moment we have all been waiting for. I will be calling out the winners from each state in random order. When your name is called, please wait, and one of our escorts will usher you to the podium to receive your award." Marines in full uniform stepped forward and stood before the stage; they would be the escorts for the evening.

Since he would not be calling in alphabetical order, Marty hoped she would be first because she could hardly stand the excitement. She had kept her drinking to a minimum so she could absorb what was actually happening and remember this moment for the rest of her life.

All the winners at the tables around the Texas table were men, and Marty was interested in what kind of businesses they ran and what their journeys had been like.

Marty wasn't keeping track of how many states had been awarded, but she was excited to see how many women were receiving them. It seemed like her turn would never come. She felt like the RNC had made a mistake and somehow forgotten her. She was dead wrong.

Tim took her hand and whispered in her ear, "The best was left for last."

Newt Gingrich asked for the President to take the podium. Marty's heart sank, because her name had not been called and it appeared they were at the end of the end of the ceremony. President Bush walked to the podium and welcomed everybody saying, "I am very happy to see such a lively crowd of Republicans, I only wish Larua could have joined me. Tonight is special on many fronts, but most of all, because this is the first time in the history of this event that the award will be given to a woman."

Marty's ears perked up and excitement started to build as she thought, "Could I be that woman?"

President Bush continued, "It is a very special person who will be receiving the award because she has not only broken through the glass ceiling but the concrete ceiling. She has reached the pinnacle of her career after fighting so hard in a male dominated arena. Join me in congratulating Marty Bledsoe!"

Marty thought she would faint when the President called her name. Tim squeezed her arm and said, "You've got this, kid. You deserve every minute of it; I told you they were saving the best for last."

One of the marine escorts was suddenly at Marty's side, ready to escort her to the podium. President Bush continued listing her accomplishments. The walk to the podium felt like the longest she had ever taken, but when she reached the stairs, she marched up them with her head held high ready to meet President Bush.

Bush gave her a big hug and said, "You are a very special woman, and being from Texas, I wanted to give this award away myself. You have set an example for other women, and surely there will be more opportunities for them as a result of your accomplishments. Your persistence and timely dedication have led to success."

He then handed her the award and shook her hand. She had accomplished the unthinkable: winning the top award ahead of all her peers in business. The crowd erupted with applause.

Marty returned to her table without her feet hitting the ground. She was the only one in the United States to have received this award, but she hoped it would mark a new beginning for women.

## THE END

www.ingramcontent.com/pod-product-compliance
Lightning Source LLC
La Vergne TN
LVHW010615100826
845148LV00014B/2979
*9798218948115*